D0538709

Earthly Delights

Earthly Delights

Rosalind Creasy

Illustrated by Marcie Hawthorne

Sierra Club Books

San Francisco

This book is dedicated to Robert,
with whom I have shared
the delights of this earth.

Copyright © 1985 by Rosalind Creasy. All rights reserved. No part of this work may be reproduced or transmitted in any form by any means, electronic or mechanical, including photocopying and recording, or by any information retrieval system, without permission in writing from the publisher.

Printed and bound in the United States of America by The Kingsport Press, an Arcata Graphics company. Color photo sections printed by Dai Nippon Printing Company, Ltd., Tokyo, Japan.
10 9 8 7 6 5 4 3 2 1

A Yolla Bolly Press Book

Earthly Delights was produced in association with the publisher at The Yolla Bolly Press, Covelo, California. Editorial and design staff: James and Carolyn Robertson, Barbara Youngblood, Aaron Johnson, and Juliana Yoder.

The Sierra Club, founded in 1892 by John Muir, has devoted itself to the study and protection of the earth's scenic and ecological resources—mountains, wetlands, woodlands, wild shores and rivers, deserts and plains. Its publications are part of the nonprofit effort the club carries on as a public trust. There are more than fifty chapters coast to coast, in Canada, Hawaii, and Alaska. For information about how you may participate in the club's programs to enjoy and preserve wilderness and the quality of life, please address inquiries to Sierra Club, 530 Bush Street, San Francisco, California 94108.

Library of Congress Cataloging in Publication Data

Creasy, Rosalind.
Earthly delights.

"A Yolla Bolly Press book."
Bibliography: p. 189
Includes index.
1. Gardening. 2. Gardening—United States.
I. Title.
SB453.C775 1985   635   84-23517
ISBN 0-87156-841-1
ISBN 0-87156-840-3 (pbk.)

Grateful acknowledgment is made to the following people for permission to reprint photographs and illustrations: pages 29 (top right) and 42, photos by Kit Anderson; page 29 (bottom), photo by Robert L. Carissimi; page 30 (top), photo by Jean Halama; page 32 (bottom left), photo by John Earl; pages 36 and 155, illustrations by Aaron Johnson; page 79, photo by Dave Schaefer, courtesy of Gardens For All; page 84, photo by John Withee; page 93, photo by Ann Cooper; page 97 (top), photo by Erwin Bauer; page 97 (bottom right), photo by Keith Logan; page 99 (bottom left), photo courtesy of Rod McLellan Company; page 131, photo courtesy of Gardens For All; page 138, illustration courtesy of All-America Selections; pages 146, 168 (top left), 174, and 177, photos by Michael Thompson; page 168 (bottom right), photo by Kate Gessert; and back flap, photo by Robert Creasy.

Camassia Leichtlinii

Captions for full-page photographs: page ii, herb vinegars at Caprilands in Coventry, Connecticut; page iv, Rosalind Creasy's pleasure garden in northern California; page 44, Karla Patterson of the Morton Arboretum in Lisle, Illinois; page 76, a beautiful example of Hopi blue corn, strawberry popcorn, and the result of cross-pollination between sweet corn and Hopi blue corn; page 146, Joe Gessert is looking for fish in the backyard water garden; page 158, this Park Seed Company demonstration garden shows that many flowers and vegetables can be grown in a small area; and page 174, Kate and Sarah Gessert are harvesting from their cottage garden.

Contents

Introduction

Imagine that you get out of bed one summer Saturday morning and *don't* say to yourself, "I guess I'll have to spend two hours mowing and edging the lawn, and, darn it, the roses need spraying, and the hedge needs clipping again." Instead, you wander, with a cup of tea in hand, out onto the back patio to see if the kiwi vine has set fruit or if any strawberries are ripe enough to put on your cereal. While out in back you smell the fragrant Damask rose that never needs spraying and listen to a woodpecker drumming in the background. As you putter around, you see which flowers are available for that night's party as well as share a moment with your child, watching a black and yellow caterpillar eat the dill and wondering if the swallowtail butterfly it is to become will stay in your yard or flit away to someone else's.

Sound idyllic? Maybe too much so to be convincing? Before I present my case for this livable garden, let's take a look at the bottom line: the financial and emotional toll modern landscaping fashion exacts. Today's typical yard—with its traditional, large lawn, its mandatory evergreens across the front of the house, and its few street trees—if shored up with a sit-on mower, electric trimmers, and bags of fertilizers and herbicides, or a maintenance service that brings in all that stuff, is one of the most unrewarding, resource-consuming, and expensive yards imaginable.

Locked into this vision of what a yard should be, homeowners don't realize that their landscapes are costing them thousands of dollars a year—not only in expenditures but in losses resulting from poor solar design. These barren yards "cost" us money by failing to lower air-conditioning bills by shading south walls from the summer sun and by failing to cut our heating bills with well-placed evergreens that serve as windbreaks. Further, these yards saddle us with any number of boring, repetitive chores and yield very little pleasure—not to mention their failure to produce food and flowers for the table.

Gardeners of this traditional style are more apt to spend their time trying to figure out why the lawn has dead spots or what disease afflicts the roses than enjoying a bird's song or taking pleasure in the progress of the native wildflowers they saved from the snowplow's blade last fall. In this all-too-typical scenario, our yards have become just one more set of chores, right up there with cleaning the oven and changing the oil in the car, one more source of worry, and one more drain on the pocketbook. Thus, Part One of this book encourages readers to pull back and let the natural habitat be part of the garden. Instead of continually trying to enforce an artificial man-made system, it encourages you to design your garden more in concert with nature and the habitat that existed before your garden was installed. A number of different approaches are explored. For instance, homeowners in the Midwest and parts of the Northeast and Northwest, where meadows and prairies are indigenous, can enhance a small lawn with a meadow or prairie garden, thus cutting down on maintenance and giving the family an area to enjoy the parade of seasons. In forested habitats, yards that carve out woodland gardens require less maintenance too, and the owners can watch the bustle of nest building and enjoy a cool place to sit on a steamy August day. Gardeners on the West Coast can cut down on watering by putting in a jewel-colored chaparral garden in a silvery setting.

Part Two portrays the garden as an ark. The concept is Noah's Ark, with a difference: the ship is made of soil, not wood, and the beings ensconced there against the dangers of the outside world are primarily plants and seeds, not animals. Readers will find information on how to identify both wild and domestic species in danger and how to save them, both as growing plants and as seeds. These ideas are so fundamental and simple they have formed the basis of our agricultural heritage from time immemorial, but restating them in the context of the modern world inspires excitement and new resolve. Heritage societies and seed banks are forming in many communities across the country, and they are circulating species of flowers, vegetables, and fruits that have been out of common view for a long time. Readers of this section will find many practical suggestions for turning their gardens into lush and fruitful arks.

In Part Two we look more closely at the damages already sustained by the web of life with which we share the world's resources. In the process this section addresses the gardener whose bent is to roll up the sleeves and *work*. Whereas restoring and maintaining natural ecosystems require a relative lack of intervention compared with traditional landscaping methods, actively seeking solutions to existing environmental problems takes energy and involvement.

The problem Part Two tackles is the most critical of all the environmental issues we face: the permanent extinction of more and more species of plant and animal life, resulting from pollution and the dismantling of natural ecosystems. Many forms of life are already gone forever, but countless more are in danger of being lost. Gardeners with the interest and energy—and knowledge, too, for one must be able to identify and nurture an endangered species either in the wild or in the garden in order to save it—can make a tremendous difference in this regard. Gardeners interested in coming aboard this ark can choose among gardens filled with heirloom vegetables such as 'Jacob's Cattle' bean and purple broccoli; wildlife habitats filled with plants for birds and butterflies; heritage rose gardens bursting with roses called 'Maiden's Blush', 'Austrian Copper', and 'Belinda'; and a windowsill orchid garden filled with chartreuse, crystalline yellow, and showy bronze blooms.

Part Three, Pleasure Gardens, is the bold effort to take on the Puritan work ethic. The guiding principle there is the restatement of a famous presidential quote: "Ask not what you can do for your garden, but what your garden can do for you." The idea is that gardening need not be an obligation or a chore; it can be primarily a source of relaxation, enjoyment, even therapy, if we toss out the "thou shalts" and create exactly the kinds of gardens we want. Thus, cooks can plant gourmet gardens —even further, Chinese cooks can plant Chinese gourmet gardens; Italian cooks, Italian gardens. Gardeners who want the garden to help save money can put in a moneysaving garden. Parents who long to spend some time relaxing with their small children can make children's gardens with their offspring; and those of you who long to kick off your shoes and just plain enjoy life in the garden can put in a pleasure border filled with fragrance, bright colors, succulent foods for the table, and edible flowers. Forget fashion, forget the tyranny of the lawn and shrub border. Think about what you like to do in life and plant a garden to match.

I have a dream, a dream that the American yard will be redefined. Instead of a piece of mandatory lawn stretching from sea to shining sea, choices will be made. On the one hand, homeowners who want less involvement will choose gardens that require less maintenance and yards that serve as depositories for native plants and animals. On the other hand, homeowners who glory in gardening will choose to use their energy to nurture some of the endangered wild and domestic plants. And, finally, I dream that the yard will be redefined to be an opportunity to partake of the earth's greatest treasure: the rich diversity of species, of which we are only one.

PART ONE

ECOSYSTEM GARDENS

What did the land look like before your home was built on it? Was it a meadow filled with milkweed and goldenrod? a pine forest alive with the chatter of jays? a prairie or a sage-filled chaparral? Did an elk migration path cross your front yard? Did a rare lady's-slipper grow there, or a native Franklinia tree now never found in the wild? Whatever your land looked like once upon a time, it is certain that workers showed up one day with a shovel or bulldozer and leveled part of that area to bare dirt. How much they leveled varied from lot to lot, but no matter how little earth was disturbed to situate the house, the first step had been taken toward creating a suburban, people-oriented ecosystem and permanently altering the existing natural environment.

Occasionally, after a house is built, the surrounding flora is allowed to close back in around it, but that is certainly the exception. In most cases new landscapes are designed in keeping with prevailing fashions. And for the better part of the past two centuries, those fashions have favored "immigrant" plants and human-made hybrids—varieties created by breeders—over naturally occurring species. Thus, while most American yards contain a tree or two left over from the undeveloped days, such as a maple, magnolia, or oak, the majority of plants in the American garden never would have grown there naturally. Our yards are melting-pot ecosystems: hydrangeas, rhododendrons, and chrysanthemums from the Orient; apples, irises, and daffodils from Europe; acacias and eucalyptuses from Australia; gladiolus and even so-called Kentucky bluegrass from Africa. All are immigrants.

Most of us, although surrounded by such people-created, artificial ecosystems, have never evaluated their function or questioned their long-term impact on our lives and the environment. When our population was smaller and life was less complex, when gasoline was cheaper and chemical pollution was not a problem, when numerous habitats and species weren't endangered, there were fewer reasons to question the validity of the "exotic" approach. Now, however, people of many different disciplines, philosophies, and lifestyles are questioning the appropriateness of some of our traditional landscaping techniques and styles.

In response we are developing new landscape techniques, sometimes referred to as *natural gardening* or *ecoscaping*. These developing responses cover a great range of involvement with the natural, occurring habitat. For example, some homeowners are choosing to modify a traditional yard by including a few native plants; some are choosing to enhance and modify an existing habitat, combining the natives with a small lawn and a flower border; still others are enjoying the challenge of trying to reestablish, as closely as possible, a meadow, prairie, woodland, or chaparral area, whichever habitat would have been there eons ago. Though these approaches vary in labor intensity, they all take as their theme the native ecosystem that existed prior to human development of the land.

Enhancing and modifying the existing habitat instead of putting in an artificial one have some practical advantages for the homeowner. Usually the more closely the landscaping reflects the natural landscape, the less maintenance and expense for the homeowner. Also, by eliminating many of the nagging chores, such as having to spray the roses or water the begonias and the lawn, you will have more time for a pleasurable involvement with your yard. As an added bonus, because so much of suburbia is building-coded into conformity, natural landscapes can give you a yard where the plants, and even the style, can be as different as you want from your neighbors'.

Certainly, on a day-to-day level these reasons for "going native" are convincing enough. In addition, consider the long-range values if you feel strongly about the direction things are taking on a global scale. Will our grandchildren have to take their children to nature centers to view a few of the rare remaining robins, say, or monarch butterflies? We ourselves must already depend on books to see and show our children a substantial number of plant and animal species that are gone forever. By landscaping with an eye to restoring and preserving our natural ecosystems, and by stemming the tide of bluegrass that threatens to stretch from coast to coast, we can, with appropriate alterations to create niches for ourselves, make safe corners here and there in which indigenous plants and animals can thrive. Each household's contribution may be small, indeed, but the combined effort could mean the continued existence of many habitats and the living things that depend on them.

Native Plants

There is a shopping center called The Oaks in our neighborhood. It derived its name from the magnificent native oak trees incorporated in the design. The oaks could not take the urbanized treatment and they died, so the center is now just a barren expanse of asphalt. In New England I've seen the Blueberry Farms housing development, where there's nary a blueberry bush to be seen. I've begun to think of these earthy touches by the developers in their project names as nostalgia, at best, and, at worst, as nasty jokes on the victims of their zeal. Native plants and the animals that depend on them are disappearing at the hand of

NATIVE PLANT COMMUNITIES

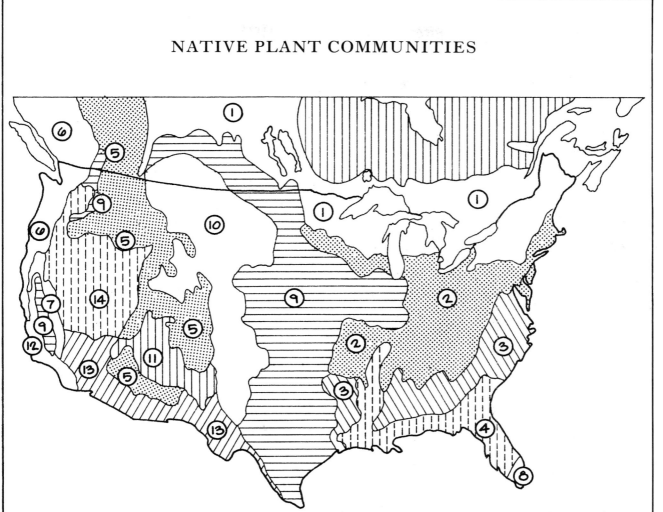

1. Northern mixed forest
2. Eastern deciduous forest
3. Southeastern mixed forest
4. Outer coastal plain forest
5. Rocky mountain forest
6. Pacific forest
7. Sierra cascade forest
8. True subtropical
9. Tall-grass prairie
10. Short-grass prairie
11. Pinon-juniper woodland
12. Coastal chaparral
13. Warm desert
14. Cold desert

To choose the native plants for your ecosystem garden, you must first determine in which kind of habitat you live. Look over this map to see which ecosystem is dominant for your area. As you can see, the primary ecosystem of the Northeast and the Northwest is a woodland. But just knowing you are in a woodland ecosystem is not enough; there are hardwood maple forests as well as coniferous forests. Also, interspersed among woodland areas are clearings we call meadows: some are boggy, others are dry.

The ecosystem of the greater part of our heartland is the prairie. Prairie ecosystems become more and more arid the farther west they are, so prairies are described as dry-land or wet-land prairies. While some of the arid West could be classified as desert—complete with cactuses and roadrunners—there, too, one finds great variation. For instance, there is scrub oak chaparral as well as a similar habitat of pinon pine and rabbitbrush. Desert areas, marshes, bayous, tropical rain forests, and beachside sand dunes represent other ecosystems in this country. For further detailed information about your own eco-system, consult the books recommended at the ends of the chapters on ecosystem gardens and inquire at local nurseries, universities, and native plant societies.

man at an alarming rate. Every year greater numbers are added to the endangered species list. The United States already lists 1,400 endangered species.

To ponder the reasons that native plants have been ignored and underutilized is an interesting philosophical exercise. After all, European gardens are filled with California poppies, lupines, Michaelmas daisies, Monterey cypress, penstemons, columbines, Oregon grape, and Virginia creeper. It appears that on both sides of the Atlantic the status of those who could afford landscaped yards was enhanced by the inclusion of exotic imported plants.

Perhaps that's less than generous. It may well be that the early settlers who came to this country were a bit homesick and wanted to be surrounded by plants from their homeland. Or perhaps they brought with them plants they knew how to grow. For whatever reason they favored the imports, it's particularly ironic that Americans have never paid much attention to native species, since we have one of the most varied floras from which to choose.

Our great diversity of climates and geology has created an incredible array of plants: from lady's-slipper orchids, sword ferns, and blueberries, through yuccas and magnolias, to the giant redwoods. Geography is one reason for our great diversity, but another is weather. North America was less affected by the ice ages than were many other parts of the world. The advancing ice stopped short of our southern waters, enabling our plant species to survive and, after the ice retreated, reestablish their old territories. As a result, we have one of the world's most diversified floras.

Note: It is critical to choose the right plant for the climate. The zone map on page 186 will help you select plants that will grow successfully in your yard. The map, adapted from a map prepared by the U.S. Department of Agriculture, delineates hardiness zones and is used consistently by nurseries, seed companies, and almost all gardening books.

Because native plants have been undervalued for years in this country, information on growing them has been relatively sparse and suppliers have virtually ignored them. When natives were stocked, there were often problems: some are hard to germinate, nobody knew how to grow some of them, and, most important, consumers didn't buy them. Nursery people in the West had additional problems because many western natives are particularly challenging to grow in containers because they are usually drought tolerant with deep root systems that cannot withstand being confined or overwatered.

The new interest shown by home landscapers in environmental quality, resource conservation, and cost effectiveness, as well as gardeners' boredom with overdressed petunias, has kindled a nationwide interest in native plants. People concerned about maintenance costs and gardening time are attracted to native plants because, as a rule, once established, these plants can be easier to care for than many of the imported or hybridized varieties. They have evolved and adapted to native soils and climates—certainly no one visits the wild black-eyed susans or jack-in-the-pulpits with a watering can and a bag of fertilizer. In addition, such plants have struck their own balance with the indigenous insects and diseases, so they rarely need spraying. (They do, of course, have problems with introduced pests such as gypsy moths and Japanese beetles.) In fact, natives are sometimes considered hard to grow because most don't like to be fussed over, watered, and fertilized: they sometimes die from too much care.

Furthermore, an "official" expertise in natives is growing apace. Botanists, conservationists, and government officials concerned about our diminishing plant communities have become interested in preserving some of the nation's diverse habitats, be it a section of virgin prairie or a part of The Everglades. They have funneled energy and money into learning about native plants and disseminating information on them. Consequently, quite a bit of material is now available from government agencies. Help is also available from interested horticulturists, universities, native plant nurseries, and—probably of most value to the home gardener—numerous native plant societies whose plant mavens can advise home gardeners on what to grow, where to plant it, and how to take care of it. These dedicated native plant lovers will sometimes even share seeds and plants with gardeners who are sure to plant and care for them.

Working with Native Plants

From the new wealth of material, we can glean a few basic guidelines for working with native plants.

1. Even though a plant may be native to your area, it may not do well in your yard. Your soil could be quite different from that of your neighbor only a few hundred feet away, as could be the drainage and exposure to cold winds. Get to know your particular mini-climate. Compare notes with other gardeners in your area. Do the same plants grow well? Does your yard have any unusual characteristics? For instance, if your yard is situated on a hill or in a gully, if your soil seems much more acidic, sandy, or claylike than surrounding properties, have an extension agent or local university help you choose native plants for your yard.

2. You can't always determine what is native to your area by observing what is growing nearby because many species brought from other parts of the world have escaped and taken up lodging in our woods, meadows, and grasslands. The discussion of weeds in this section describes many of the introduced plants. Books about native plants for your area usually tell which plants are indigenous and sometimes describe introduced species.

3. Some native plants have very specific growing requirements and are not domesticated like some of our commonly grown garden plants. (Analogous is the situation of keeping wild and domestic animals: the koala bear eats only a specific type of eucalyptus, but domesticated cows and sheep, long selected by humans for their adaptability, eat different kinds of grasses from all over the world.) Many of our domesticated plants are adaptable to a wide range of conditions; still others have been selected to be compatible to human environments, whether it be air pollution, road salt, or lawn-water runoff. However, many native plants are very adaptable: Jerusalem artichokes, goldenrod, coreopsis, gaillardia, Douglas fir, and Lawson cypress, for example, grow over a wide range. Still, thousands aren't adaptable. Again, therefore, I emphasize that you must do your homework and find out the specifics about your garden—its soil, climate, and drainage—and get the native plants that are suited to it.

4. If you want many different native plants in your yard, you will have to seek them out. Often you will have to obtain them from friends or contact native plant nurseries for plants and seeds.

5. Do not dig up a plant in the wild unless it is being threatened in some direct way, such as by a building project or a snowplow. Do not collect seeds without permission, and never take all of the seeds: leave some for the habitat. (See the information in Ark Gardens on how to avoid purchasing plants that are illegally taken from the wild and the information in the section on how to rescue native plants.)

Unless you live in an unusually pristine area, even with the most conscientious of efforts you will not be able to exactly duplicate what was naturally there. The chances are that when your house and driveway went in, topsoil was removed or compacted; or maybe a concrete mixer was emptied into the ground, and the diluted cement changed the pH; or perhaps a marsh was drained. In addition, you or previous homeowners may have applied herbicides or planted invasive species such as honeysuckle, barberry, or Bermuda grass, all of which can make returning the site to its previous condition a formidable task.

Another important consideration is that *you* have specific requirements; your yard is for you and your family as well as for providing a habitat for other living things. Perhaps you have a nonnative wisteria or European birch that gives you great visual pleasure or shades the house in summer, a plant you would miss if you took it out. Houses surrounded by prairies, meadow grasses, or chaparral need a lush, green, fireproof buffer. Homes completely surrounded by woodlands, with trees planted up to the house, can be cold and make you feel confined. In addition, babies can't crawl in the arctostaphylos, and you can't play badminton in the wild strawberries.

Setting Your Goals

To begin your landscape project, you must set goals. Your goals could be any or all of the following: to have a low-maintenance yard, to save money, to help preserve some of the area's vanishing plants and animals, to learn about your environment, to spend more time relaxing with the children, to use fewer resources, to have a more unusual yard. Be aware when setting your goals that many of these goals are interdependent. Also, you should realize that these landscapes will need more maintenance at the beginning, before the plants fill in, than they will after they are well established. In order to save money, you may want to spend time locating seeds in the wild instead of buying them.

Another part of the planning process is to develop realistic expectations. Meadows pictured on calendars and seed packets knock your eyes out with what's called "lollipop color," great swaths of red or orange poppies, mounds of butterfly weed and coneflowers, or fields of

blue lupines. However, in real life, those spectacular shows are very unusual; to duplicate them takes more effort than to have just an average meadow. If you want to have great swaths of color in your meadow, you will have to mow it occasionally, weed out particularly invasive species, overseed it with a wildflower mix, and probably water it. (Nature generally gives her biggest flower shows only in wet years.) Meadows and wildflower gardens aren't the only landscape situations where we like pizzazz. Most of us also like natural landscapes to have a big show. Instead of purely green woodland walks, we like banks of blooming laurel or azaleas; a small waterfall is nice too. Traditionally landscaped yards, whether filled with exotics or natives, usually have more color and more plants of unusual shapes than natural ones because the plants have been chosen to stand out. Nursery catalogs offer an array of plants that have the biggest, showiest blooms and the most varied colors. Let's face it, most of us like nature with the volume turned up. Hence, one decision you will have to make is how much of a purist you want to be. Your options range from populating your yard with only indigenous species to putting a few particularly showy native shrubs and trees around your lawn.

Maintenance

Maintenance is synonymous with "putting your finger in the dike of succession." No matter what degree of involvement you choose to have with your yard, there are a few basic concepts that these more natural forms of land-scaping involve. Ecosystems of all types change —they are dynamic. Homeowners try to stop the process: we put our fingers in the dike, and we call it "maintenance." We pull out the oak seedling that the squirrel planted, we prune the ivy, and we mow the grass. However, if people were removed from the earth, a hundred years from now our houses would be obliterated by ivy, oak trees, honeysuckle, and thousands of other species. When uninterrupted by humans, over the years a meadow often becomes a woodland, a young pine forest might mature to a mixed-hardwood forest, and bogs fill up to become meadows. This phenomenon is called *succession.* The implications of succession for the homeowner who wants a natural landscape are many. For instance, if you want to convert your lawn area to a woodland, you are trying to compress a long evolutionary process into a few years. You will have to make some compromises and make sure a number of soil and moisture conditions that support woodlands are available, as well as wait to put in shade-loving, understory plants until the trees have grown for a while. Those homeowners who want a wildflower meadow or prairie will have to control the encroachment of shrubs and trees. Almost all homeowners will have to contend with many herbaceous plants, most of which we refer to as weeds. Herbaceous plants can be considered the pioneers of ecological succession; they are usually the first species to grow in a cleared or disturbed area. Some are indigenous, but, increasingly, particularly in suburban areas, they are introduced species that are even more aggressive than native ones. These aggressive annual and perennial plants

Kudzu, *Pueraria lobata,* from Japan has become a "green cancer," often growing seventy-five feet in a season, smothering hundreds of native plants.

need control in any meadow, prairie, woodland, or arid-climate garden until you have established a fairly stable habitat.

Planning Your Landscape

Scan the map and determine your ecological region; then, to get your first taste of landscaping with natives, turn to the chapter in Part One that most closely corresponds to your region.

In most parts of the country, slightly modifying your existing yard by adding a few native plants takes little more effort than going to your local nursery and asking someone there to recommend a selection. A more ambitious effort, taking out some of the lawn and replacing it with a section of meadow or prairie plants or augmenting your arid hillside with some choice chaparral plants, will require some research, into both your own ecosystem and the sources for some of the more unusual plants.

However, it is this middle ground that I have outlined in detail in The Woodland Garden, The Meadow Garden, The Prairie Garden, and The Chaparral Garden.

To make much more ambitious changes in your yard, such as replacing large parts of your nonnative yard and closely approximating what was there originally or starting out with a piece of bare ground, you will need much more direction than this book can give. For help on such large-scale natural landscaping, you will need to acquaint yourself with information on plant communities, concepts of climax vegetation and succession, and basic botany. In addition, you will need information on drainage, soil types, and basic design. Armed with some basic botany and microclimate information to identify your original environment, you can examine your particular goals and landscaping needs in the context of your native ecosystem.

Use the book list at the end of this introduction to Part One to do some reading on your particular region. Don't be discouraged; helpful people and information are available.

Weed or Native Plant, Friend or Foe?

Ecoscaping is not just an excuse to let your yard "go to the dogs." Untended land, particularly in suburban areas, fills up with blown-in newspapers, sow thistles, and old tires and can become a neighborhood nuisance. Ecoscaping is an active process, and even though it is low maintenance, it requires some well-timed tasks and supervision to make your yard attractive. It is *low* maintenance, not *no* maintenance. An important maintenance task, as any gardener knows, is guarding against those intrusive species known as weeds.

Weeds, weeds, weeds. Ask people to name a weed and the odds are overwhelming that they will name the dandelion. How many hours of toil, tons of herbicides, and millions of dollars have gone toward obliterating this cheerful survivor. Herbicide advertisements and media emphasis on pristine lawns and flowerbeds have focused our attention on the dandelion and other herbaceous plants that invade lawns, flowerbeds, and waste areas. Sadly for wild plants, this media blitz has given us a very limited view of weeds.

What is a weed anyway? The usual definition is: Any plant that is out of place. But when people think of weeds, they usually think of them as "out of place" in a lawn, a garden, or an agricultural setting. Well, many of them are, but we must think of weeds in a more global way; that is, plants that are out of place in a wild ecosystem. The fact is that millions of acres of natural areas are as overrun with weeds as are the most weedy vegetable gardens or lawns. Our mindset about weeds, that is, only plants that are out of place in cultivated areas, is so strong that I've unnerved friends and relatives while driving or walking through so-called wild areas by giving a running patter of the names of all the invading species, nonnative plants that have escaped the confines of a cultivated plot. Suburbia, too, is overrun. Half the trees, it seems, that abut the famous Merritt Parkway in Connecticut are escaped ailanthus—the tree in the title *A Tree Grows in Brooklyn*, which came from China. Square miles of the Southeast are covered with what's referred to as the "green cancer," kudzu. This vine, imported from Japan, first as an ornamental, then by some well-meaning government officials who used it for erosion control, can sometimes grow seventy-five feet in one season. It climbs over and smothers whole stands of trees and obliterates habitats. There are virtually no controls, chemical or biological, and kudzu marches along "eating up" the South.

Scotch broom, Japanese honeysuckle, and lantana are plants that evoke strong emotions. For many gardeners they elicit pleasure because they bloom so effortlessly; to a member of the native plant society or to a farmer they are often a scourge. Homeowners, gardeners, nurseries, landscape architects, even park department personnel have long examined only one side of the equation—is it pretty? The other side of the equation has to be: Does the plant benefit or hurt any aspects of the environment? The ornamental gardener has no idea what mayhem some of his treasured plants cause. Just as many rural dog owners don't know that their pet dogs run in packs occasionally and kill deer and the neighbors' chickens, so home gardeners are oblivious to the damage done by some of their plants. Farmers use tons of herbicide trying to control escaped lantana in Florida and honeysuckle in the Northeast; square miles of native plants and the animals that depend on them are annihilated because gardeners are enchanted by purple loosestrife, as well as many, many more lovely but—to the native species—deadly plants. With many of the weed species it is like closing the barn door after the horse is gone; already hundreds of square miles of lantana, kudzu, and Scotch broom are out of control. The aim here is to help contain some of these species and not add to the problem. Take purple loosestrife, for example; yesterday a catalog arrived in my mail advertising wildflower seed mixes. There it was—touted as a great, easy-to-grow wildflower for meadows and landscaping use— 250,000 seeds for $10. And it was in most of the seed mixes as well. I shudder when I think of the hundreds of acres of native vegetation and the species that depend on them that will be obliterated!

Home gardens are not the only source of invasive weed species. Agriculture and the government have unwittingly done their share —maybe even our beloved Johnny Appleseed is suspect because there are thickets of wild apples crowding out their neighbors in parts of the Northeast. Everyone must share the responsibility for altering native habitat, and because there are so many millions of us now, everyone, including the home gardener, must take responsibility for halting the spread of invasive species.

When I was visiting the Citrus Arboretum in Orlando, Florida, I was told that almost half of the herbicide used in Florida citrus orchards is used to control lantana. Since lantana is such a noxious weed, you would think that it would not be sold in nurseries. Not so! In the West, native plant societies schedule weekend outings to kill rampant Scotch broom, and while members are out trying to eradicate the plant, they drive past nurseries selling it. Farmers in the East battle Japanese honeysuckle. Again, you would think honeysuckle would not be sold in nurseries, but it is!

The numbers of introduced ornamental plants that are growing out of control are legion: English ivy is climbing up into trees and covering the ground in the Northwest; Oriental bittersweet, sometimes called the "strangler of the North," marches across the Northeast; Scotch broom and pampas grass infiltrate miles of California's most scenic route, Highway 1; and in the warm climates of Florida and Hawaii, where freezing temperatures do not cut down the invading armies, the most notorious weeds, like hybrid lantana, Brazilian pepper, casuarina, and melaleuca (punk tree), go berserk. It is estimated that fully 16 percent of the plants in southern Florida are nonnative! Some of these often-attractive invaders are so ubiquitous that they have been given deceiving local names; for instance, Brazilian pepper is commonly referred to as "Florida holly."

The sad fact is that although we have been conditioned to see dandelions in the lawn, pigweed in the vegetable rows, and grass in the farmer's field as negative, we have been conditioned to see Oriental bittersweet, multiflora roses, and Scotch broom as beautiful; and almost as if to prove their value, you can go to the nursery and pay $5 for one in a container. We must not continue to compound the problem; otherwise, the habitats of this nation will lose their diversity.

Above The cajeput tree, *Melaleuca quinquenervia,* which was introduced from arid Australia many years ago now grows rampant in Florida. Often the trees are only two to three feet apart, completely obliterating square miles of native plants in the water-rich environment of The Everglades. While this problem has existed for years, only recently has the sale of the cajeput tree been prohibited in Florida.

Left In contrast, melaleuca varieties growing in arid California are welcome, well-behaved additions to the landscape. Because individual species behave differently in different ecosystems, it is imperative that you become acquainted with the plants that can become a problem in your area.

Controlling Weeds

If you are gardening with a thought to the environment, the issue of escaped plants becomes very tricky. Environmental gardening often means choosing plants that need little coddling with fertilizers, irrigation, and pesticides. (If you are gardening on a city lot, far from any natural vegetation, the problem of which plants become problems is moot; but if you are adjacent to a wild area, the problem is one that should give you cause to do some research.) The problem is that some plants that are easy to grow are *so* vigorous that they become a problem in themselves. Therefore, one of the questions you should ask yourself before you choose a plant for your yard is: Does it grow *too* well? You will have to judge at what point a vigorous grower becomes a rampant weed that crowds out native vegetation in your area. To determine that, look around and try to identify some of the introduced species you see. It is difficult to find people who are well informed and can advise you about local invasive species, although some local extension agents and university environmental studies people may be able to give you an idea. Most nurseries and seed companies, in my experience have been hair-pullingly frustrating to deal with on the subject. They are either oblivious to the problem or will say, "Hey, that's business. If I don't sell Scotch broom in California, someone else will. The public wants it."

Here are some guidelines for approaching the problem of identifying and controlling weeds.

1. *Very* carefully examine recommended plant lists that are circulated by well-meaning agencies and organizations. The water department, for example, publishes lists of drought-tolerant plants, but on the list will be plants such as Scotch broom, pampas grass, and pennisetum grass, all of which are very invasive species. Organizations interested in birds often publish lists of species that provide shelter and food for birds. Many of the serious pest plants, while they do provide food for birds, are spread by birds and crowd out native plants that are food for butterflies, bumblebees, and small mammals. Frequently listed are such offenders as multiflora roses, blackberries, Oriental bittersweet, Brazilian pepper, and honeysuckle. In both of these examples, unfortunately, the people putting together the lists were looking only at one part of the environmental problem.

2. Beware when a garden book warns you that a particular plant may seed itself and become a pest. These plants should be used only with discretion.

3. Examine the composition of a wildflower mix before you order it. Does it contain the seeds of any problem ornamentals?

4. Look around your garden and see if you have any plants that are creating a problem.

5. Plants don't have to be exotic to become a problem. Some of this country's native plants, such as cattails and milkweed, can become invasive if they are planted in certain areas of the country or near a well-tended garden area.

6. A plant such as Brazilian pepper, which is invasive in Florida, can be well behaved in another climate, in northern California, for example.

Green Invaders

I have put together a list of some of the worst offenders for different parts of the country. It is by no means comprehensive, and many plants will respond differently from one area to another. Therefore, some of the plants on this list may be all right in your yard but not in most. Aside from avoiding the plants on this list, the most important thing you can do is to be aware that some of the lovely plants you see around you every day, when seen from a global point of view, make the lowly dandelion a pushover.

Northeast, Middle Atlantic, and Parts of the Midwest

Japanese barberry, *Berberis Thunbergii*
Japanese honeysuckle, *Lonicera japonica*
Multiflora rose, *Rosa multiflora*
Oriental bittersweet, *Celastrus orbiculatus*
Purple loosestrife, *Lythrum Salicaria*
Yellow bedstraw, *Galium verum*

Northwest

Bracken fern, *Pteridium aquilinum*
Cattail, *Typha latifolia*
English daisy, *Bellis perennis*
English ivy, *Hedera Helix*
Foxglove, *Digitalis purpurea*
Goldenrod, *Solidago canadensis*
Ground ivy, *Glechoma hederacea*
Himalayan blackberry, *Rubus procerus*
Hypericum, *Hypericum calycinum*
Oxeye daisy, *Chrysanthemum Leucanthemum*
Periwinkle, *Vinca major*
Scotch broom, *Cytisus scoparius*

Gulf States

Bermuda grass, *Cynodon Dactylon*
Brazilian pepper, *Schinus terebinthifolius*
Kudzu, *Pueraria lobata*
Lantana, *Lantana* hybrids
Punk tree (cajeput tree), *Melaleuca quinquen-ervia*
She-oak (ironwood), *Casuarina equisetifolia*

Southwest

Acacia, *Acacia melanoxylon,* plus many other species
Bermuda grass, *Cynodon Dactylon*
Eucalyptus, *Eucalyptus,* many species
Fountain grass, *Pennisetum setaceum*
Himalayan blackberry, *Rubus procerus*
Ivy, *Hedera,* many species
Pampas grass, *Cortaderia jubata*
Scotch broom, *Cytisus,* most species

Many Parts of the Country

Ailanthus (tree of heaven), *Ailanthus altissima*
Bamboo, running types
Chicory, *Cichorium Intybus*
Horsetail, *Equisetum hyemale*
Japanese knotweed, *Polygonum cuspidatum*
Morning-glory, *Ipomoea,* most species
Purslane, *Portulaca oleracea*
Watercress, *Nasturtium officinale*

Though attractive, foxglove has become a pest plant in the Northwest.

HOW TO RESCUE NATIVE PLANTS

Sometimes you hear about proposed demolition and/or construction in areas where native plants still thrive. A rescue effort can often save a number of the plants. The following are a few guidelines.

1. The most effective tool for saving native plants is an informal organization and a hotline. In the absence of a full-scale group effort, an individual can still be very effective.

2. Keep your eye on prime native habitats. Also, check city planning schedules for proposed development. Try to look over the site as soon as possible to determine which, if any, species are in danger. The sooner you make your assessment, the more options you have.

3. As soon as you know of a proposed development, contact the developer, express your concern, and offer to organize the plant-saving effort, or find someone to do it if you can't.

4. Once the developer's cooperation is assured, contact your local native plant societies, garden clubs, 4-H, and other interested organizations.

5. If you are experienced with rescuing native plants, you can show others how to do it; if you aren't, find someone who is. Saving plants is not just a matter of going into the woods or a meadow with a shovel. When possible, collect seeds of plants that are too large to be moved.

6. Help develop an informational flyer on digging up, transplanting, and caring for natives in your area; and seek an organization that can distribute the flyers to interested people.

Join the individuals and organizations all over the country who are providing a valuable service for the environment and future generations by saving endangered native plants and who have the bonus of enjoying these plants in their own gardens.

Trillium

Sources of Information

Books

Bruce, Hal. *How to Grow Wildflowers and Wild Shrubs and Trees in Your Own Garden.* New York: Alfred A. Knopf, 1976. Valuable cultural and source information. East Coast oriented from an environmentalist's viewpoint. This text includes an encyclopedia of wildflowers and their sources.

Diekelmann, John, and Schuster, Robert. *Natural Landscaping, Designing with Native Plant Communities.* New York: McGraw-Hill Book Co., 1982. A basic text necessary for informed natural landscaping. It covers in detail how to re-create stable plant communities. Useful primarily for the Northeast, Midwest, and Northwest.

Holm, LeRoy G. et al. *The World's Worst Weeds.* Honolulu: The University Press of Hawaii, 1977. A technical description of agricultural weed problems.

Koopowitz, Harold, and Kaye, Hilary. *Plant Extinction—A Global Crisis.* Washington, D.C.: Stone Wall Press, 1983. The best book for concerned homeowners. It gives extensive information about our endangered ecosystem and speaks extensively about invasive weed species.

Kruckeberg, Arthur R. *Gardening with Native Plants of the Pacific Northwest.* Seattle: University of Washington Press, 1982. A great resource for northwesterners, this book includes growing information for the Northwest as well as detailed information on species for the garden.

Mohlenbrock, Robert H. *Where Have All the Wildflowers Gone?* New York: Macmillan Co., 1983. An excellent discussion of the wildflower problem.

Ortho Books, William H. W. Wilson. *Landscaping with Wildflowers and Native Plants.* San Francisco: Ortho Books, Chevron Chemical Company, 1984. A most valuable and up-to-date book covering in detail most of the many ecosystems in this country. The book contains numerous lists of native plants to choose for your landscape as well as information on how to plant and maintain them.

Smyser, Carol A. *Nature's Design.* Emmaus, Pa.: Rodale Press, 1982. A very detailed primer for designing your yard around native habitats and with native plants.

Consumer Note

When is a native not a native? Like "organic" or "natural," the term "native" has sometimes been abused. Too often nurseries and, especially, mail-order firms will call a particular seed mix a native wildflower mix, for example, when often as many as half of the seeds in the mix are native to Europe, not to the United

States, much less to a particular region. Nurseries will often sell plants from another part of the country and call them natives. Theoretically they are natives, but if the reason you are growing natives is to help preserve a habitat or to provide food for indigenous species of animals, these so-called natives may not be appropriate. Plants from other ecosystems are fine, but they don't usually further the goals of habitat preservation. If you want truly indigenous species, you must research your ecosystem and determine the precise species you want.

Be aware that hybrids of native plants exist. Some of our natives have been bred for home gardens and have few of the characteristics of their hardy cousins. For example, I purchased some particularly showy mimulus for my drought-tolerant flower border one year. In our area mimulus grows wild and blooms all summer with no watering, but the mimulus I had bought continually wilted. I investigated and found out that they were mimulus hybrids and needed practically as much water as most garden flowers. So, again, natives aren't always natives.

Moist meadow lily

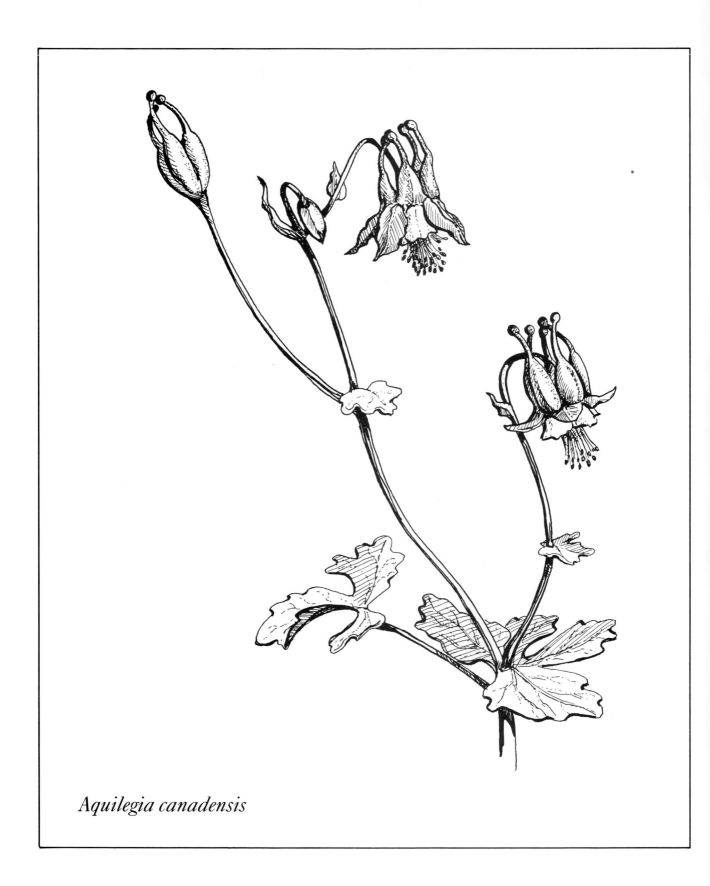

Aquilegia canadensis

Chapter 1
The Meadow Garden

When I was a child living in a Boston suburb, the neighborhood was filled with houses and lawns, but across the street from us we were lucky enough to have a small vacant lot. Certainly, we enjoyed tumbling on the lawns and playing croquet, but some of my fondest memories are of exploring the vacant lot. (Isn't it interesting how people-centered the word *vacant* is.) In the lot—actually a meadow —we looked for ripe milkweed pods, pulled them apart, and rubbed the silky fibers against our noses; then we blew the plumes into the wind and watched them float away. Also, we watched monarch butterflies, picked golden-rod, collected sumac pods, and made secret hideaways under the arching branches of the willow. In the evenings we caught lightning bugs and put them in a jar. That vacant lot is no more. Now there is a white house with a lawn, two yews, six junipers, one dogwood, and a maple tree.

Today there are fewer and fewer vacant lots. Driving across the country you see, mile after mile, suburban lawn abutting suburban lawn. Some of the lawns are small; others cover an acre or two. But that is changing as more people begin to question the overemphasis on

lawns. Less and less are people willing to spend two or three hours a week tending their lawns; furthermore, homeowners are questioning the value of spending money on fertilizers and water, spreading questionable chemicals on the soil around their homes, and wasting resources. (Annually Americans use 3 million pounds of nitrogen fertilizer on their lawns; that's as much as all of India uses on its agriculture in a year.) And, finally, people are becoming bored with the sterility of lawns and concerned about the obliteration of the habitats of native plants, animals, and birds.

One alternative to the large lawn is the meadow. You've heard the term *meadow,* but what is it really? Botanically, a meadow is a somewhat stable plant community that is dominated by grasses. It is associated with a climate that has quite a bit of rain, as compared to a prairie that is usually found in drier parts of the country. A meadow's composition changes with soil type, climate, and available moisture. A meadow in a boggy corner of Oregon will be very different from a meadow on a dry hillside in New Jersey.

Humans, too, change the makeup of a meadow. Unmanaged meadows in many suburban areas are filled primarily with introduced weeds, brush, young trees, and, sometimes, wind-blown trash. Managed meadows in suburban areas, on the other hand, can require fairly little maintenance and still be exciting areas that are filled with black-eyed susans, poppies, sumac, columbines, milkweeds, or other indigenous species—all changing with the seasons.

If you have a fairly large piece of property or a yard in an area where all the yards aren't trimmed to military precision, you can consider converting some of your yard to a meadow. But first consider the following limitations of a meadow.

1. Some municipalities have so-called weed ordinances, which usually state that homeowners cannot let their lawns grow taller, say, than four or eight inches. These old laws were enacted before there was an awakening to the environmental ramifications of square miles of lawns. The object of these laws was to give cities controls over negligent homeowners and to prevent fire hazards. These laws are still on the books in some areas, and you might encounter them. Be aware, though, that these types of laws have been successfully overturned by concerned citizens.

2. Remember that meadow areas are usually one of the first steps in the natural succession of ecosystems. If not maintained as a meadow, unless it's in a very boggy area, the expanse will probably eventually become a woodland.

3. Once established, meadows are full-sun habitats. Trees shade out the sun-loving plants and are appropriate only on the periphery.

4. Meadow areas are not interchangeable with lawns. They are occasionally appropriate in small areas, but generally they function as a supplement to a small lawn area.

5. Meadow grasses and flowers produce more pollen than a mowed lawn and should be avoided if anyone in your family has severe allergy problems.

If your yard is sunny, if the neighborhood is appropriate, and if allergies aren't a problem, the advantages of a meadow are numerous, as indicated by the following list.

1.Meadows planted with indigenous species of grasses and flowers attract native birds, small mammals, butterflies, and other insects.

2. Meadows change dramatically with the seasons, providing much more visual pleasure than a huge lawn does and a valuable learning experience as well.

3. Meadows require very little maintenance. They need only annual mowing to keep the woody species from taking over and occasional weed control to keep them looking neat. They also need little watering—none if nature is cooperative at seeding time and if flowers are not expected all summer long in arid climates.

4. Meadow flowers and grasses will give you a long season of flowers, both fresh and dry, to cut and to enjoy in the house.

5. Meadows that are well maintained and generously overseeded will give your yard a boost of spectacular color with very little effort.

If you live in a part of the country where the meadow is an appropriate ecosystem, particularly in the Northeast and the Northwest, creating one will be an exciting project. If you live in the Midwest, see Chapter 3 for a variation on the meadow, the prairie.

Planning and Preparation

Meadows are delightfully variable: each one is unique in some way. Even when meadows are planted with the same seed mix, different climates and soils and the germinating seeds of the species that were originally growing there will combine to give you an unpredictable show; and that's half the fun. The process of putting in your own meadow is fairly straightforward. First, choose a sunny area for your meadow; it can be as small as one hundred square feet or as large as several acres. See the accompanying plan for ideas on how you might situate your meadow. Notice that the meadow is away from the house. As a rule, this is recommended because: (1) trees are often needed near the house for protection from wind and sun, (2) meadows cannot function the way lawn does as a place to play ball or to sunbathe, (3) meadows are usually inhabited by mice and other small mammals that would not be welcome in the house, and (4) meadow grasses in dry periods can become a fire hazard. Notice also that the vegetable garden and orchard are fenced and separated somewhat from the meadow garden. The reason for that is to try to minimize visits from the meadow's inhabitants and to cut down on the damage they might inflict.

Once you have decided where you will put your meadow, ask yourself the following questions:

1. Which kinds of wildflowers and grasses are native to my area? (If you need help, refer to the resources at the end of this chapter.) Successful meadows can be created also by sowing seed mixes that are not blended especially for your area, but you will probably not attract as many indigenous insects and birds, and fewer species will reseed themselves. If you don't have the time or inclination to "fine-tune" your meadow to your area, an interesting alternative is to try the Meadow in a Can, a colorful, easily grown, premixed selection that is distributed by Clyde Robin Seed Company (the address is given in the resource section at the end of this chapter).

2. What is the drainage like? If the soil stays moist for much of the year, you must choose species that tolerate poor drainage.

3. How much seed shall I order? Measure the area to be seeded and consult a seed catalog. To give you a rough idea, Clyde Robin, the "granddaddy" of wildflower nurseries, recommends the following amounts: for an area that has some trees and shrubs, sow five pounds of seed per acre; for a clear area, eight pounds per acre; and if you want a big, lush show, try fifteen pounds per acre.

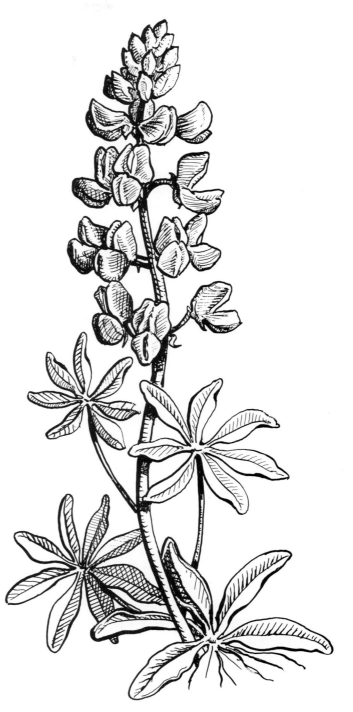

Lupinus nanus

4. Shall I look for bargains when shopping for seeds? Buy good seeds. There is no surer way of wasting money in gardening than to buy cheap seeds. Good wildflower seeds, costing $20 to $30 per pound, may seem expensive; but, relatively speaking, they're not. Seeding is the least expensive way to landscape an area; with seeds, more than with most other things in life, you get what you pay for. The reason for the expense is that many of the wildflower seeds must be collected in the wild—an expensive operation. In contrast, clover, which is often used as a cheap filler in wildflower mixes, can be field grown and picked by machine; therefore many of the inexpensive seed mixes are mostly clover seeds combined with only a few seeds of the more desirable species. In addition, many of the cheaper mixes contain more easily obtained European flower seeds, not natives. That may not be a problem if you're not a purist, but the native flowers are more likely to attract our native insects and birds, and they are more likely to reseed themselves year after year. In addition, they are less likely to become weeds that crowd out native vegetation. Weed seeds and poor germination rates can also be a problem with cheap seeds. If your budget is tight, seed more lightly and let the flowers reseed themselves. Another option, of course, is to collect your own seeds. (To do this, you must be aware of where the flowers are growing, when they bloom, and when the seeds of each species are ripe. You must beat the birds to the harvest and catch the seeds before they fall to the ground.)

5. How do I prepare the soil? If the proposed meadow area is quite weedy, it is best to till up the soil a few weeks before planting, and keep the area well watered. This procedure will germinate the weed seeds. Before you plant the flower seeds, you should plow under the newly sprouted weeds. If you have the time and patience to repeat this procedure, you will probably give your flowers a very strong start and dramatically cut your weeding chores.

How to Plant a Meadow

Steve Atwood at Clyde Robin Seed Company recommends the following procedure for planting a meadow. If possible, plant in the fall; that gives the flowers enough time to get established and set seed the next fall. If you plant in the spring, the chances are that you will have to reseed the next year.

If you have an existing lawn area, plow it under; remove as many weeds and stones as possible, then rake the area. If you are overseeding an existing meadow area and you want a good flower show, remove a lot of the grasses. Most wildflowers have a hard time competing with grasses, particularly if the grasses are already established. (A word of caution: Don't just cast the seeds on hard, dry ground; you will just feed the birds a very expensive meal.) Rough up the soil. Use a spade if the soil is heavy or packed down. If it's sandy soil, rake it well. Before you plant, mix your seeds with coarse sand: five parts of sand to one part seed. This mixture allows you to spread the seeds more evenly. Sow the seeds, then either water very gently with a fan spray that will softly puddle the soil over the seeds or rake the area very lightly. Try not to cover the seeds with more than one-eighth inch of soil. Once the seeds are sown, you must keep the area moist for two or three weeks. Water lightly if it does not rain. (Fall plantings are often accompanied by rain, a work-saving advantage if you live in an arid climate.)

This landscaped yard provides for people as well as for some native plants and wildlife. People live snugly, protected from winter winds by evergreen shrubs and trees. A fence ensures that most of the harvest of tomatoes and lettuce and other vegetables ends up on the kitchen table, not in some bunny's mouth. The orchard is planted with dwarf trees so that netting can easily be put in place for protection from birds. A path and sitting area were added to the meadow so that sunny hours can be spent enjoying the business of living that meadows so embody. In addition, you may be able to pick black-eyed susans, tiger lilies, and goldenrod; watch birds gather seeds and nesting materials; and see butterflies sip nectar from the ever-present flowers.

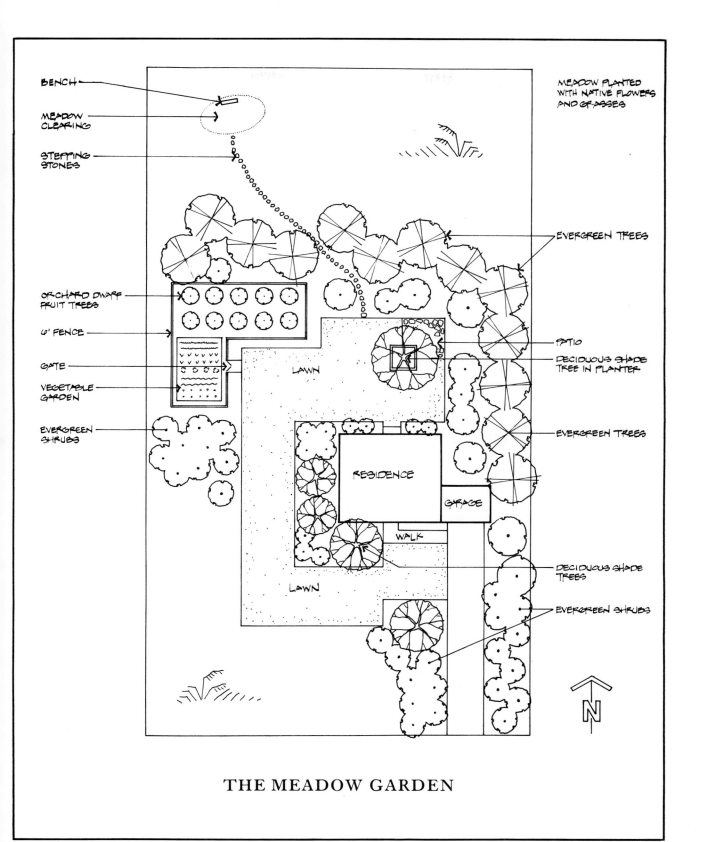

BENCH

MEADOW CLEARING

STEPPING STONES

MEADOW PLANTED WITH NATIVE FLOWERS AND GRASSES

EVERGREEN TREES

ORCHARD DWARF FRUIT TREES

6' FENCE

GATE

VEGETABLE GARDEN

EVERGREEN SHRUBS

LAWN

PATIO

DECIDUOUS SHADE TREE IN PLANTER

EVERGREEN TREES

RESIDENCE

GARAGE

WALK

LAWN

DECIDUOUS SHADE TREES

EVERGREEN SHRUBS

N

THE MEADOW GARDEN

How to Maintain a Meadow

If you live in an arid climate and want flowers well into the summer, you will have to irrigate the meadow area often enough to keep the flowers growing well. Weeds can be a problem—are they taking over or becoming an eyesore? If they are, you will have to weed by hand or turn the field over and start again *after* germinating the weed species and turning the area over once more.

Most wildflower mixes contain both annual and perennial flowers. The annuals will bloom the first year, but the perennials usually take two years to bloom. The perennials are well worth the wait because they continue to bloom year after year, and generally their show increases each year (particularly when the flowers you choose are native to the area).

A meadow is not no maintenance; it is *low* maintenance. To keep the area a meadow, you must mow it at least once a year, in the fall after the flowers have seeded themselves. Get a mower that will mow six to ten inches off the ground. Often you can rent one. This type of machine is sometimes called a *flail mower*. Because weeds in the area will start to take over, plow up the area every five years or so and resow it. To avoid being disappointed, you should keep in mind that annual flowers give the biggest color show the first year after planting. Although they will reseed year after year, usually they don't reseed as heavily as you sowed them originally. If you have chosen an all-annual selection, you may want to reseed from year to year. If you choose a mix that is mostly perennials, it will have some color the first year and gradually more color each year thereafter.

Clockwise from top left Instead of a large lawn, part of this yard has been planted with a wildflower mix. Sitting on the deck, lemonade in hand, one can enjoy up close the daily changes in a mini-meadow.

Meadow seed mixes that will create a meadow such as this one are available at many nurseries. Several reliable sources of seed mixes are given at the end of this chapter. Even though the mixes often contain many nonnative flowers, they can be an easy way to start a meadow.

One of the stars of a meadow garden is often the black-eyed susan.

Above This beautiful prairie setting is enjoyed and maintained by David Kropp and Ray Schulenberg, prairie enthusiasts. It is seen here in late spring, with pink and lavender coneflowers among the emerging grasses. Through summer and fall it will be filled with the wandlike seed heads of five species of grasses and the blooms of sixty varieties of flowering prairie plants. Kropp and Schulenberg harvest about six gallon jarfuls of prairie seeds every year and share them with others interested in prairie restoration. (Landscape design: The Kropp Company)

Left Butterfly weed, *Asclepias tuberosa,* is a spectacular inhabitant of much of this nation's prairie. It is a star performer in a border of prairie flowers and in a more natural planting of prairie grasses and flowers.

Opposite, clockwise from top left The Littauers' chaparral garden in the spring is filled with bright blue native ceanothus varieties and yellow dendromecon, as well as some drought-tolerant African species of yellow and white daisies. (Landscape design: Rosalind Creasy)

Fremontodendron is one of the showiest of the West Coast native shrubs.

Drought-tolerant chaparral gardens can be supplemented with showy water-loving annuals during the winter rainy season. Here illustrator Marcie Hawthorne enjoys the orange calendulas among the drought-tolerant permanent plantings of the purple spikes of pride of Madeira, *Echium fastuosum;* old-fashioned bearded iris; and African daisies, *Osteospermum.* (Landscape design: Rosalind Creasy)

Sources of Information

Books

Brooklyn Botanic Garden Handbooks. *Gardening with Wild Flowers*. No. 38. Brooklyn, N.Y.: Brooklyn Botanic Garden. How to incorporate wildflowers in your garden. This handbook is available for a small charge from Brooklyn Botanic Garden, 1000 Washington Avenue, Brooklyn, NY 11225.

Crockett, James Underwood, and Allen, Oliver E. *Wildflower Gardening*. Alexandria, Va.: Time-Life Books, 1977. A general view of the subject, with specific information on a number of wildflower species.

The next four entries are useful guides for identifying your own flowers or those in the wild; use these guides for pleasure and for seed collecting.

Duncan, Wilbur H., and Foote, Leonard E. *Wildflowers of the Southeastern United States*. Athens, Ga.: University of Georgia Press, 1975.

Niehaus, Theodore F., and Ripper, Charles L. *A Field Guide to Pacific States Wildflowers*. Boston: Houghton Mifflin, 1976.

Peterson, Roger Tory, and McKenny, Margaret. *A Field Guide to Wildflowers of North-eastern and North Central North America*. Boston: Houghton Mifflin, 1968.

Rickett, Harold William. *Wild Flowers of the United States*. 6 vols. New York: McGraw-Hill Book Co., 1966-70.

Nurseries

Larner Seeds
P.O. Box 60143
Palo Alto, CA 94306
Specialists in native and naturalized seeds of New England and California.

Midwest Wildflowers
Box 64
Rockton, IL 61072
Specialists in midwestern wildflowers.

Painted Meadows Seed Company
P.O. Box 1494
Charlottesville, VA 22902
Specialists in East Coast wildflowers.

Plants of the Southwest
1570 Pacheco Street
Santa Fe, NM 87501
Southwestern native flowers and Indian varieties of vegetables that are adapted to the Southwest. Catalog $1.

Clyde Robin Seed Company
P.O. Box 2366
Castro Valley, CA 94546
The granddaddy of wildflower seed companies in this country has been in business for seventy years. It carries a large collection of wildflower seeds from all over the country and will select for your area. Catalog $2.

Opposite, clockwise from top A reed fence with a Japanese-style gate adds mystery and design while daffodils add a splash of color to Robert and Joyca Cunnan's woodland garden.

The entry to the Cunnans' garden shows how a graceful path through native trees, enhanced with flowers and a small clearing, can carve an inviting setting for a home. (Landscape design: Robert and Joyca Cunnan)

Woodland anemones such as this one, *Anemone lancifolia*, brighten up a woodland garden.

Cornus florida

Chapter 2
The Woodland Garden

Woodland gardens can provide serenity, privacy, a feeling of seclusion, protection from winter winds, and a cool, dappled retreat on hot summer days. Woodland gardens also provide a never-ending drama. Paths that lead into woodland gardens invite strolling and exploration. Patios, porches, and kitchen windows that have a view of a woodland garden are never boring places to be. Busy chickadees flit to and fro, jays scold their neighbors, chipmunks dash from tree trunk to tree trunk, the days are full of meaningful activity—the business of living.

Woodlands take many different forms: hardwood forests of rock maple and ash in Vermont, loblolly pine forests in the South, ponderosa and pinon pine in the West, and bigleaf maple and hemlock in the Northwest. Woodland gardens are appropriate to a large part of this country; their native range includes most of the northern regions of this country as well as more southerly mountainous areas. In keeping with the philosophy of this book, I'm stressing woodland gardens that represent the indigenous habitat of your own property. While it may be interesting to create a woodland garden in a grassland habitat, the point here is to

restore or preserve native habitats so that indigenous species can better reproduce themselves. In addition, woodland gardens in a woodland habitat will benefit the homeowner because naturally occurring habitats usually require less maintenance.

Woodland gardens are amazingly flexible. If you live in an existing woodland area, you can carve out and enhance it to meet your needs. If the ground has been laid bare or if you are removing a large lawn, you can create a woodland area with patience and skill. The size of your property is not a limiting factor; you can create woodland gardens in an area as small as twenty feet by twenty feet or in an area as large as twenty acres. If you have a small area, you may want to follow some of the Japanese gardening concepts. Traditional Japanese gardeners have long captured the essence of woodlands in miniature gardens. In contrast, if you have a large area, you would do well to control only the area near your home and along paths leading through the woods.

Woodlands are complex systems. When mature, they usually include a canopy of tall, shading trees; understory trees, young trees and those trees that have adapted to shady conditions; a shrub understory, both tall and short shrubs; and herbaceous shade-loving plants. Another characteristic, which is important to homeowners who want to carve a garden area in a woodland, is the varied plant community that develops at the edges of woodlands and forests. Areas on the periphery of a forest, next to a meadow, for example, or in a clearing, usually have a number of sun-loving herbaceous plants, shrubs, and small trees. These plants give you, the garden designer, a wide variety of plants from which to choose when making your garden.

There are a number of elements that will influence the way you design a landscape based on a woodland habitat. If you are starting from scratch, you must analyze the existing conditions and assess what must be done to approximate the conditions you want. If you are modifying an existing woodland area, the main issues are how to make the existing area provide protection for the house from wind and sun, how to make the area suitable for your household, and how to create a lovely garden. One further consideration is how to create a garden that will benefit the plants and animals in the area. This chapter includes an example of how to design a specific woodland garden. Also, Chapter 6 includes information that may be helpful.

Planning and Preparation

The first steps for creating a woodland garden are similar no matter where you live, whether your garden is large or small or whether you are starting from scratch or altering an existing woodland. To begin, you must set and analyze your goals and make an inventory of what is on the site.

First, goal setting. What do you want from your garden? Is it mainly for viewing from the house? for entertaining? for a children's play yard? or mainly for food production? Only you know the answer. Woodland gardens are a source of year-round interest and beauty; woodland gardens offer hospitable surroundings for a patio or barbecue area. In addition, few gardens can give children such a rich area for exploring and playing. If food gardening is one of your goals, however, you must plan your garden carefully, and if you have a small yard, the combination of woodland and food production may be impossible. Woodland gardens are primarily shade gardens, and most food plants need full sun.

Next, the inventory. What do you have to work with? If you are modifying an existing garden, identify first those plants that you want to preserve. Which special features make the area unique and beautiful—maybe a rock outcropping, a gnarled old oak near the house, a marsh, or a stream? While you are taking inventory, include an analysis of the property's soil characteristics and drainage and exposure; all these factors dictate what your woodland garden will be like. Make a map of your property, locating all the features on it so you will be able to work with them later.

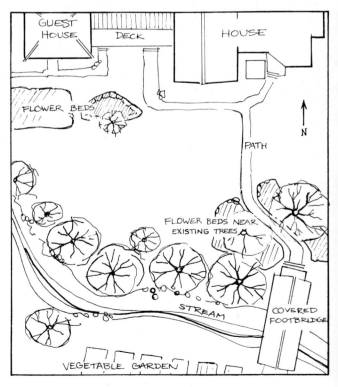

What needs to be removed? Do some of the trees block a beautiful view or obliterate what little winter sun your home receives? Are some of the trees and shrubs really invasive weeds that should come out? Has the existing landscaping outgrown its bounds? Are the yews starting to lift the roof? If providing habitat for wildlife is one of your goals, are there a number of modifications that should be made (see Chapter 6)?

How does your garden area function? Does the present wood area, or proposed one, provide a windbreak? Are there deciduous trees that shade the house in summer? If the woodland area is large enough to be managed to provide wood for the fireplace and stove, is that one of your goals? If so, you will need to choose trees that are suitable.

At this point you may need further direction. Either obtain some of the books recommended at the end of this chapter or hire a professional designer who works with native plants to help you create your garden.

Modifying Existing Gardens

If your home has been built in an existing woodland, your landscaping job will be quite different from that of someone who is starting from scratch. Yours will be a job of sculpturing and molding an area to please your eye. Here are a few guidelines.

1. Create some open spaces in the woodland area. These spaces can be created by lawn, groundcovers, paths, patios, or all four. Most homeowners prefer some of the open area to be adjacent to the house because it provides a protected sitting area. A grove of trees very near the house can give you a feeling of claustrophobia.

2. Create paths that lead both you and the viewer's eye out into the woods. Clear some of the trees and shrubs from beside the walks for flowering woodland natives that can be enjoyed by the family as they meander down the path.

3. Thin out the canopy near the open areas and remove some of the trees to allow more sun for flowering shrubs and small trees such as mountain laurel, serviceberry, dogwood, native rhododendron, and low-bush blueberry. Concentrate the flowering plants in the thinned-out areas and near places where people enjoy sitting or walking or where they can be viewed from the house.

Starting from Scratch

If you are starting a woodland garden from scratch, it is necessary to take into account many of the aesthetic considerations mentioned above. In addition, you will probably have to do some research to find out what would have grown there naturally. Instead of inventorying your yard, you must inventory the surrounding woodland vegetation to see what is indigenous. If woodlands in your area have been obliterated, you can get information from the library, the local native plant society, and the university extension service.

When you plan to create a woodland garden from scratch, it is crucial to realize that you are trying to compress into a few years what nature takes generations to achieve; therefore, you have to be aware of how you must help the process. Some general guidelines for planning a new woodland garden are given below.

1. Examine the soil and drainage because they dictate which plants you can choose.

2. Trees, shrubs, and woodland wildflowers need a soil rich in humus. If the soil in your garden has been depleted of organic matter over the years through ignorance or neglect, you will have to improve the soil with compost before you start planting, then you will have to mulch the area for the first few years.

3. A new woodland garden is produced in stages. Only after a number of years will the area be shady enough that you can plant many of the shade-loving, forest-floor dwellers. Until the trees fill in, plant sun-loving wildflowers.

Trees for Woodland Gardens

Trees for Northeastern and Midwestern Woodland Gardens

Acer species. Maples of all types give substance and grandeur to woodland gardens. The real star, however, is the sugar maple with its spectacular fall foliage that is famous throughout the world. Maples are excellent grove trees that provide not only fall color but food and shelter to woodland animals.

Amelanchier species. Most serviceberry species are colorful and provide berries for people and birds.

Betula species. Birches are graceful grove trees that provide food for birds, beautiful bark, and fall color. Few woodland gardens are as graceful as those that feature birches. To show them off to their best advantage, combine them with some of the native evergreens.

Cornus species. Dogwoods, one of our woodland favorites, provide colorful flowers and food for birds. Place them near paths and clearings so their flower show can be fully appreciated.

Diospyros virginiana. The persimmon is a handsome tree that provides food for birds and people, as well as a show of orange foliage and fruit in the fall.

Fraxinus species. Many of the native ashes are very attractive woodland trees that give vibrant fall color. When grown in woodland gardens instead of formal yards, their propensity to reseed themselves nearly ceases to be a problem.

Ilex species. Many of the native hollies are extremely attractive, and they provide food for birds. Since they are evergreen, they can give protection from the wind in the winter.

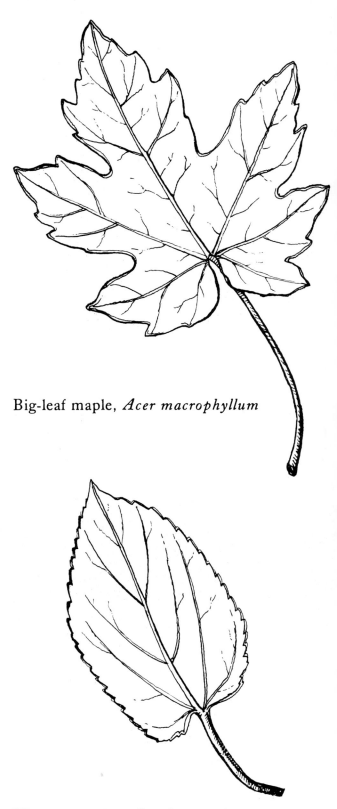

Big-leaf maple, *Acer macrophyllum*

Western catalpa, *Catalpa speciosa*

Juniperus virginiana. Attractive evergreen that attracts birds and protects homes from the wind.

Liquidambar Styraciflua. Sweet gums are stately trees that are beautiful in groves or by themselves. They give handsome fall color in the southern regions of the East Coast.

Liriodendron Tulipifera. Tulip trees are vigorous, handsome trees that are effective in groves or by themselves.

Pinus species. Many of the native pines form the basis for striking woodland gardens. Use their evergreen foliage to advantage as a windbreak for winter winds. To keep the pine-tree woodland garden from being too dense and dark, thin it near your living areas and the paths and plant the transition areas between the pines and the open areas with flowering shrubs, small trees, and deciduous plants that have showy fall foliage.

Quercus species. Most of the oaks are suitable for woodland gardens and are all-time favorites of wildlife.

Trees for Western and Northwestern Woodland Gardens

Cornus Nuttallii. Pacific dogwoods are a special treat, particularly in the Douglas-fir and hemlock woodland garden, where their white or light pink blooms are a contrast to the dark green background foliage of the conifers.

Populus tremuloides. Quaking aspens are to the West what birches are to the East, ornamental clumping grove trees of outstanding beauty. Aspens are water lovers and should not be planted near sewer lines or in small yards; give them room to spread, and feature their clumping tendencies in your woodland garden. To take full advantage of their spectacular fall foliage, combine them with some of the native evergreens.

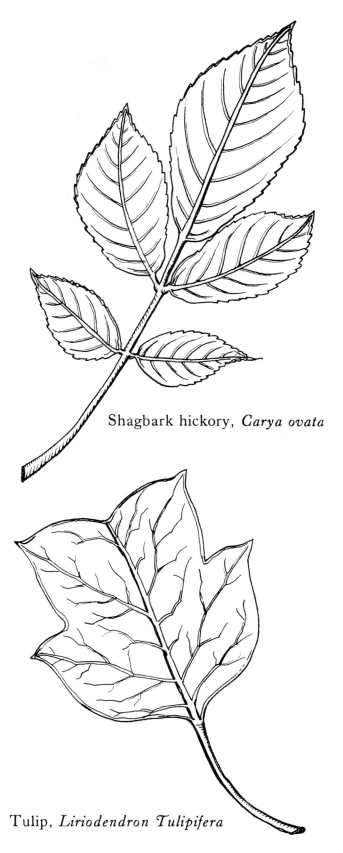

Shagbark hickory, *Carya ovata*

Tulip, *Liriodendron Tulipifera*

Pseudotsuga Menziesii. Douglas firs are large, graceful evergreens that are suitable for large properties. Woodland gardens using these beauties can be filled with shade-loving native ferns, flowering shrubs, and perennials.

Sequoia sempervirens. Few woodland gardens on the West Coast rival the redwood forest. If redwoods are native to your area and if you have lots of room, plant groves of redwoods. They grow quickly, and within a few years you can put in the shade-loving sorrel and native sword ferns.

Tsuga heterophylla. This native hemlock has a wide range and is a handsome evergreen that needs lots of room to spread. Make it the basis for a dramatic woodland garden.

By looking at the illustration of Jean Richardson's garden, you can get a feel for how a pleasure garden can be carved out of a natural woodland.

When the Richardsons bought the lot fifteen years ago, it was covered with native woods; namely, sugar and red maples, ash, black cherry, white pine, hemlock, buckthorn, shad, beech, and canoe birch. When building, the Richardsons left as many of the trees as possible but cleared an area around the house to create a garden. Lawn areas and many different ground covers are used to form the design lines and to allow a view of the wooded areas. Jean has put in a small vegetable and herb garden that is near the house and that takes advantage of the available sunlight. Other nonnative plants around the house include azaleas, rhododendrons, coral bells, ajuga, lupines, yellow primroses, pachysandra, daylilies, hybrid lilies, foxgloves, lilies-of-the-valley, sweet woodruff, snow-on-the-mountain, and violets—all give color and variety to enhance this woodland garden.

In the natural woods, among the rock outcroppings, and in a number of areas near the house are various native ferns, including Christmas fern, sensitive fern, and ostrich fern and wildflowers such as wild ginger, trillium, Solomon's seal, columbine, lungwort, wild iris, rhododendron, viburnum, myrtle, and jack-in-the-pulpit. Some of these natives have been planted; others, such as the myrtle, have migrated in on their own. All in all, the Richardsons' garden has given great pleasure to the occupants of the house while still allowing the native wildlife, both plants and animals, to have their own habitat.

Opposite The Richardsons carved a woodland garden out of native woods. They left most of the trees and shrubs in place but included a clearing where showy natives and exotics could be featured as well as a small vegetable-growing area. The result is a garden that gives joy to the owners and provides a habitat for native plants and animals. The plants include:

1. Amelanchier (shad)
2. Sweet woodruff (ground cover)
3. *Viburnum carlcephalum*
4. Weigela
5. *Viburnum tomentosum*
6. *Euonymus alata*
7. Forsythia 'Beatrix Farrand'
8. Canoe birch
9. White pine
10. Snow-on-the-mountain
11. Wild azaleas
12. Rhododendrons
13. Daylilies
14. Lily of the valley
15. Honeysuckle
16. Bayberry
17. Azaleas
18. *Malus* 'Dorothea'

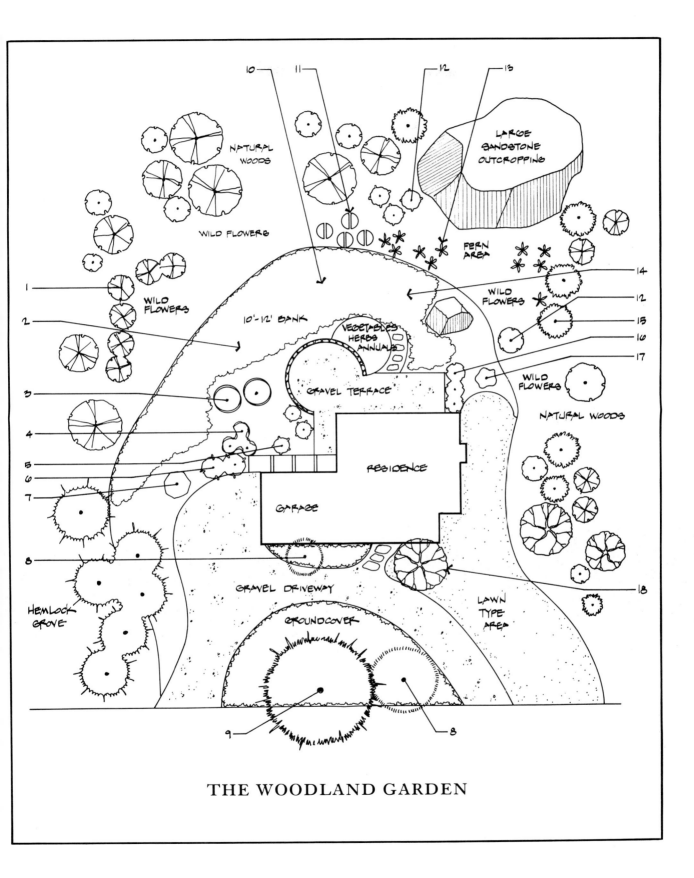

THE WOODLAND GARDEN

Jean Richardson enjoys adding vegetables and flowers to her woodland garden.

Sources of Information

Books

Bruce, Hal. *How to Grow Wildflowers and Wild Shrubs and Trees in Your Own Garden.* New York: Alfred A. Knopf, 1976. Contains good information about putting in a native garden for people on the East Coast and in the Midwest.

Du Pont, Elizabeth N. *Landscaping with Native Plants in the Middle-Atlantic Region.* Chadds Ford, Pa.: Brandywine Conservancy, 1978. A valuable resource for gardeners wanting a woodland garden on the Atlantic coast.

Kruckeberg, Arthur R. *Gardening with Native Plants of the Pacific Northwest.* Seattle: University of Washington Press, 1982. A wonderful source of information about northwestern natives, with suggestions of many plants to use in a woodland garden.

Demonstration Gardens

Garden in the Woods
Hemenway Road
Framingham, MA 01701

Ida Cason Calloway Gardens
Route 27
Pine Mountain, GA 31822

Morton Arboretum
Lisle, IL 60532

Nurseries

Forest Farm
990 Tetherow Road
Williams, OR 97544
This nursery carries native plants. Catalog $1.50.

Salter Tree Farm
Route 2, Box 1332
Madison, FL 32340
This company carries seeds of southern native trees and shrubs.

F.W. Schumacher Company
36 Spring Hill Road
Sandwich, MA 02563
This nursery carries seeds of a number of trees.

Chapter 3
The Prairie Garden

In the heartland of America lies an ecosystem that has produced an array of flowers and grasses that is more varied than that found nearly any place on earth. That ecosystem is the American prairie. A treat awaits you if you have not yet discovered the beauty of a border filled with native prairie flowers and grasses. The options range from the bright "lollipop" colors of some of the flowers to the more subdued colors and ephemeral seed heads of the mauve- and bronze-hued plume grasses. Some of these plants take care of themselves, while others are a challenge to the gardener and need tending. If you live in an area that was once a prairie habitat (nearly half the country), no matter what your gardening style or time, you owe it to yourself to enjoy a patch of prairie natives.

When Europeans first arrived on this continent, the midwestern prairies stretched for millions of square miles. Today these virgin prairie ecosystems are in such danger that most of what exists is in patches the size of a football field; and those are in jealously guarded preserves. The great expanses of bluestem and needle grass, the thunder of buffalo hooves, and the cries of prairie chickens have nearly disappeared. They have been replaced by the much-needed corn and wheat farms and cattle ranches and the less necessary bluegrass lawns. A valuable ecosystem, as well as part of our history, has been nearly obliterated.

Biologically, the definition of a prairie is a treeless expanse dominated by native grasses, some short and others many feet tall, and forbs (broad-leaved plants, usually those that flower). This definition gives little hint of the *wonders* of a prairie, however. Willa Cather defined it more poetically: the "sea of wind-blown grasses" and "the stain of crimson phlox" as far as one could see. I, a newcomer to the prairie, was most impressed with the variety of grass seed heads: some like wands, some like feathers, others like soft plumes, but all luminescent in the sunlight.

When that treeless expanse covered a great part of this country, within it different types of prairies could be discerned: the tall-grass prairies of Iowa and Nebraska, where the rainfall is heavy; the short-grass prairies of the semi-arid plains of Colorado, Kansas, and northern Texas; and the sagebrush grasslands of the cold, arid parts of Idaho and Wyoming. Right down the middle of the Midwest, where there were a number of different conditions, was a large section of mixed-grass prairie.

Homeowners interested in enjoying prairie plants or in preserving some of the endangered prairie habitat have a number of choices. For the busy homeowner who wants a small lawn or who needs grass for a play area and is looking for a low-maintenance lawn, some of the short, hardy prairie grasses such as buffalo grass and sideoats grama can be used as fairly tall, informal lawns. These lawns need mowing only three or four times a year and require little water and fertilizer. While they will never look as formal or lush as a bluegrass lawn, these "ecology" lawns are appropriate in many areas. Other low-maintenance prairie gardens are composed of borders of some of the particularly easy-to-grow prairie flowers such as coreopsis, coneflowers, and many of the grasses.

For gardeners or environmentalists who want a challenge, installing an authentic prairielike area in the yard, with all its beauty and seasonal changes, can be a consuming but highly rewarding endeavor. While prairie plantings can be fairly low maintenance when well established, the actual process of creating an authentic prairie area of half an acre or more can require much effort.

Because humans have completely obliterated the natural system, those wanting to establish and maintain an area of prairie today must contend with a number of problems. First, aggressive, introduced plants such as wild morning-glory, European oat, dandelion, and bluegrass pose a problem when you are trying to start your prairie plants. Because most prairie plants tend to put most of the first-year growth into the roots, not into top growth, their sparse leaves are often shaded or crowded out by the lush invaders. And once the prairie plants do become established, they must compete with aggressive, introduced, woody plants such as multiflora roses, Japanese honeysuckle, Siberian elm, and numerous other trees that shade the sun-loving natives.

A second problem encountered by the gardener wanting to establish a prairie is how to find out what grew naturally in the area. With so many houses, roads, and parking lots where the native habitats once were, one must do some botanical sleuthing in order to reestablish the preexisting ecosystem. In addition, the introduced exotic plants (never seen by a buffalo, of course) range from Euell Gibbons's wild asparagus to Queen Anne's lace and wild mustard.

Another challenge for the prairie restorer is dealing with local ordinances: (1) weed-abatement laws (laws that prohibit high grasses, although these laws have been overturned on many occasions by prairie enthusiasts) are a community's stubborn hold on the traditional landscaping styles that require clipped lawns and formal shrub borders; and (2) restrictions against burning. Nature maintained and protected her prairie by burning it to the ground every few years. The frequent burning killed young shrubs and trees that would have invaded and shaded out the prairie plants and helped germinate some of the prairie seeds. Burning your prairie may not be feasible because of fire regulations or because of your prairie's proximity to dwellings. If that is the case, you can compromise by mowing it every year instead and reseeding it often.

As you can see, putting in a sizable prairie and helping it become well established can be a challenge, albeit a rewarding one. Once established, prairie plantings dramatically set off every type of house, from the sod-roofed prairie house to the old Victorian mansion. In addition, instead of experiencing the boredom of a large lawn, you will enjoy day-to-day changes. Prairies offer a variety of blooms, from shooting stars and butterfly weed to tall-grass seed plumes. They invite birds, butterflies, and small mammals that are completely dependent on the prairie ecosystem.

Those who are interested in a large expanse of prairie will do well to join one of the myriad prairie preservation organizations. These dedicated people can give you information on your particular area and help you locate seeds, transplants, and even the machinery to seed large areas. Besides the "ecology lawn" and a full-fledged prairie restoration, there are two other exciting, and less ambitious, options for prairie gardening that are covered in detail in the next few pages: (1) planting a somewhat formal flowerbed with a collection of prairie grasses and forbs, and (2) seeding a flowerbed or a small section of the yard with a random mix of prairie plants from a seed packet.

Planning and Preparation

There are two types of gardens that can give you a taste of prairie gardening. They are ideal for beginners or for people with limited time. One is a prairie patch, which incorporates a small piece of mixed prairie in your yard; the other, a prairie border, is a flower border featuring individual prairie plants. Pat Armstrong, ecobiologist, longtime prairie enthusiast, and head of the Morton Arboretum Prairie Restoration Project in Illinois, has put together some basic prairie plant information on these two types of prairie gardens. The following recommendations are hers.

For both prairie gardens follow these suggestions.

1. Pick a site that gets as much sun as possible; full sun is best.

2. Most prairie plants are not too particular about soil. They will grow in rich black soil and in poor sandy soils. In addition, they can tolerate clay soil with poor drainage. Some plants are better adapted to one condition or another, however, and individual plants will have different growth habits in different soils.

3. You can obtain seeds and plants for your prairie patch in a number of ways. Get plants from friends and neighbors who can make divisions or who have extra plants. You can buy plants from some local nurseries and prairie organizations. Seeds are available at some nurseries (see the list at the end of this chapter)

and from friends, neighbors, and prairie organizations. You can collect seeds from wild areas such as those along railroad right-of-ways and public back roads. (Never take plants from an area unless you know it has been condemned for a road or a building. Native plants are best left in their native environment. In addition, never take all of the seeds of any plant, and don't remove seeds from private land or from public parks.)

4. It is best to obtain seeds and plants that have been grown near you; they will be better adapted to your local climate and soil type. Using seeds and plants purchased from a distant nursery may result in poor gardens and can introduce exotic genes into the local gene pool.

5. Plant either in the spring or in the fall. If you sow seeds in the spring, use stratified (cold-treated) seeds; otherwise, germination will not occur that spring. If you sow in the fall, you can use recently purchased or collected seeds because the seeds will stratify naturally over the winter and sprout in the spring. Seeds should be planted late enough in the fall so that weed seeds don't germinate before winter, thereby getting a head start on the prairie plants.

6. An alternative to seeding in place is buying plants of many of the species or raising plants from seeds in pots so that you can set them out exactly where you want them. This method sometimes gives the plants a head start.

7. Prairie plants have evolved in a grassland environment that is subject to brush fires every few years. (Prairie plants, as a rule, are very flammable, and for that reason should not be used directly adjacent to buildings.) Fire is a beneficial agent; the flames return the nutrients to the soil and remove the litter. For modern prairies, burning is even more valuable, especially if done in the spring, because it tends to control the exotic, nonnative weeds that usually appear earlier in the spring than the prairie plants. If you cannot burn your prairie patch,

mow it and rake it fairly clean early in the spring to allow the sun to warm up the soil. Mowing controls woody weeds and allows the emerging prairie plants to come up in full sun.

8. As a rule it is best not to fertilize prairie plants. Usually they do not need it, and fertilizer encourages weed plants.

For the prairie patch, follow these suggestions in addition to the first eight.

1. Prepare the soil ahead of time to eliminate as many weeds as possible. To do this, plow and disk it several times, giving the weeds time to germinate between diskings, or use herbicides well in advance of your prairie planting.

2. Get a mixture of seeds and plants that has been recommended by a local prairie lover, or choose from the list that appears later in this chapter.

3. Have patience. Remember that prairie plants spend their first year or two making roots. For instance, a compass plant that is seven inches high and has only one leaf usually has a tap root that is five or six feet long. Your prairie patch, therefore, is not going to look like much the first two years. (A few plants do grow from seed to flower in one season, but they are exceptions.) When most people plant a prairie, they plant a cover crop of oats or wild rye at the same time. Then, at least, they have something to look at and to keep the weeds down until the prairie plants are established.

4. Maintaining the prairie patch the first two years involves weeding and mowing. Mow the new patch when it is about three or four inches high. That will cut the flower stalks off the weeds and prevent their reseeding. It will not harm the young prairie plants because they will still be quite small when you mow. If you recognize the weeds, you can control them by hand weeding. (If you plant the prairie plants in rows, it will help you identify them and weed them.) Burning the prairie patch in the early spring also controls weeds.

For the prairie border, follow these suggestions in addition to the first eight.

1. Choose a sunny site and lay out a pleasing design. See the model drawing in this chapter. Don't make the area too wide to maintain; either make the area narrow or make a path through it, which will allow you to weed and to pick flowers.

2. Obtain the species suggested on the plan and plant them either in the spring or in the fall. Use Pat Armstrong's suggestions for placement because she has selected the individual species for their height, form, and color.

3. Keep the bed well weeded and cut off the litter in the early spring. The prairie border will probably not come into its full glory until the third summer.

Armstrong's suggestions for the prairie patch and the prairie border include only twenty-one species—there are hundreds—and are meant as a stepping-off place, not as a "forever" arrangement. She has chosen them for their ease of growing, beauty, and length of bloom, with the progression of size and bloom duplicating the show that the prairie gives. For your prairie patch, choose from the list those species that would have grown in your area naturally. You can randomly scatter the species suggested in the proportion you want. For your prairie border, follow the suggestions for species placement, making substitutions of close relatives if you cannot obtain the ones suggested. All of the plants on the list have been chosen for their wide adaptability; nevertheless, there will be some variation in their growth habits in different soils and climates. You may want to move some of them after they have grown for a few years if in your particular miniclimate they are shorter or taller than predicted.

Prairie Plants

The following plants are included in the planting diagram on page 51.

1. Big bluestem, *Andropogon Gerardii*. The tallest prairie grass, a must for any prairie gar-

den. Blooms from August to September; three to eight feet tall; colorful in the fall.

2. Indian grass, *Sorghastrum nutans*. A must for prairie gardens. Blooms from August to October; three to six feet tall; colorful in the fall.

3. Switch-grass, *Panicum virgatum*. Has large open seed heads. Blooms from August to September; three to five feet tall.

4. Blazing-star, *Liatris aspera, L. punctata, L. pycnostachya, L. spicata*. Cattaillike pink blooms appear in August; three to four feet tall.

5. White wild indigo, *Baptisia leucantha*. White, sweet-pea-like flowers. Blooms in June and July; three to four feet tall.

6. Little bluestem, *Andropogon scoparius*. Tufted, clumping, medium-size grass. Blooms in August; two to four feet tall; colorful in the fall.

7. Cream wild indigo, *Baptisia leucophaea*. Mound-producing plant. Cream yellow, sweet-pea-like flowers bloom in May; one to two feet tall.

8. Pasque flower, *Anemone patens,* var. *Wolfgangiana*. Earliest prairie plant to bloom. Lavender flowers appear in April; one foot tall.

9. New England aster, *Aster novae-angliae*. Showy prairie aster. Purple flowers bloom from September to November; four to six feet tall.

10. Yellow coneflower, *Ratibida pinnata*. Yellow blooms appear in July and August; five to six feet tall.

11. Prairie coreopsis, *Coreopsis palmata*. Prolific yellow flowers. Blooms from June to August; two feet tall.

12. Butterfly weed, *Asclepias tuberosa*. The showiest of the milkweeds. Orange flowers bloom from June to August; two feet tall.

13. Northern dropseed, *Sporobolus heterolepis.*

Little bluestem grass, *Andropogon scoparius,* and purple prairie clover, *Petalostemon purpureum*, are common inhabitants of the prairie.

Loveliest of the prairie grasses. Blooms in August or September; three feet tall.

14. Purple coneflower, *Echinacea pallida*. Flowers have drooping pink petals and rounded purple centers. Blooms in June or July; two feet tall.

15. Lead plant, *Amorpha canescens*. A prairie shrub with tiny blue green leaflets and spikes of deep purple flowers. Blooms in June or July; two feet tall.

Sideoats grama and Texas coneflower are often found together and are much more common now than the native grouse that used to inhabit much of the prairie.

16. Purple prairie clover, *Petalostemon purpureum*. Purple blooms from July to August; one foot tall.

17. Stiff goldenrod, *Solidago rigida*. Large flowering goldenrod. Blooms from August to October; three to four feet tall.

18. Prairie smoke, *Geum triflorum*. Early spring bloomer with three pink bell-like flowers that never open. Blooms from April to June; one foot tall.

19. Bird-foot violet, *Viola pedata*. Showiest of the prairie violets. Blue violet flowers bloom from May to June; five inches tall.

20. Shooting-star, *Dodecatheon Meadia*. Pink blooms appear in May or June; one to two feet tall.

21. Blue-eyed grass, *Sisyrinchium albidum, S. angustifolium, S. campestre*. Small plants with blue or white flowers. Blooms from May to June; six to eight inches tall.

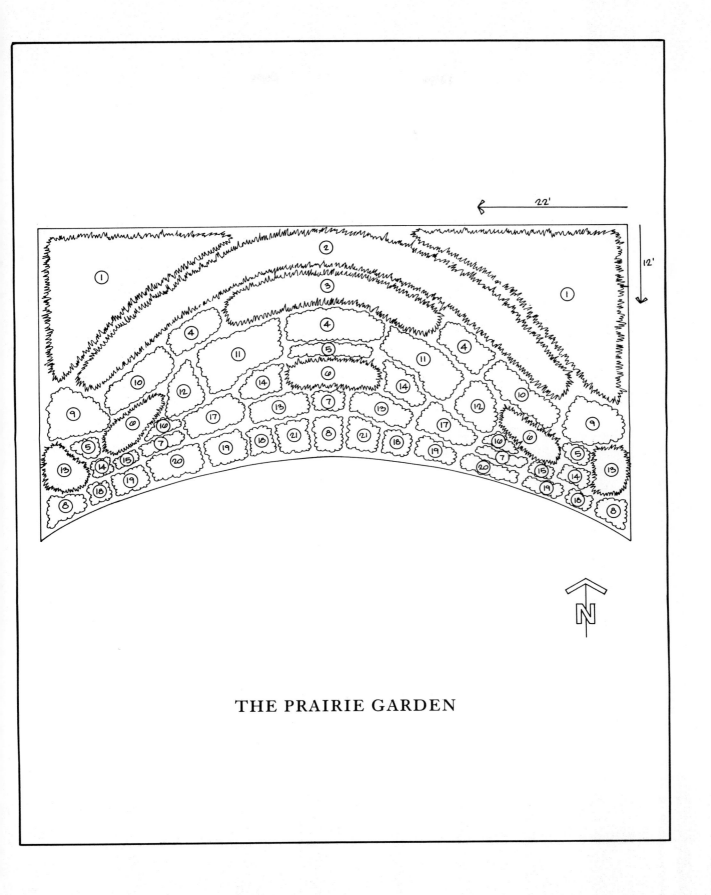

THE PRAIRIE GARDEN

Sources of Information

Books

Diekelmann, John, and Schuster, Robert. *Natural Landscaping, Designing with Native Plant Communities.* New York: McGraw-Hill Book Co., 1982. Basic information on landscaping with natural ecosystems, including prairies.

Nichols, Stan, and Entine, Lynn. *Prairie Primer.* Madison: University of Wisconsin—Extension, 1978. A marvelous little book for beginners that has all the basics.

Rock, Harold W. *Prairie Propagation Handbook.* Hales Corners, Wis.: Milwaukee County Department of Parks, 1981. This basic text is necessary for those who are interested in maintaining a prairie garden.

Smith, J. Robert, and Smith, Beatrice S. *The Prairie Garden.* Madison: University of Wisconsin Press, 1980. A useful book that describes in detail seventy native prairie plants and how to use them in your yard. In addition, it details how to collect seeds, raise your own plants, and maintain a prairie.

Demonstration Gardens

Alfred L. Boerner Botanical Gardens
Wehr Nature Center
5879 South 92nd Street
Hales Corners, WI 53130
This botanical organization has been very active in prairie restoration, has a prairie project, and can offer extensive information on prairie gardening.

Morton Arboretum
Lisle, IL 60532
The Morton Arboretum has a wonderful stand of prairie that is open to the public, as well as a very well informed staff.

Shaw Arboretum
P.O. Box 38
Gray Summit, MO 63039
A wonderful prairie to walk through. It's about a half hour's drive from St. Louis. The arboretum offers information on prairies.

Nurseries

Wildflower and Prairie Grass Seeds

Midwest Wildflowers
Box 64
Rockton, IL 61072

Prairie Restoration
P.O. Box 327
Princeton, MN 55371

Stock Seed Farms
R.R. Box 112
Murdock, NB 68407

Wehr Nature Center
5879 South 92nd Street
Hales Corners, WI 53130
Sells only mixed prairie seeds.

Windrift Prairie Nursery
Route 2
Oregon, IL 61061
Catalog 30 cents in stamps.

Native Grass Seeds

L.L. Olds Seed Company
P.O. Box 7790
Madison, WI 53707

Sharp Bros. Seed Company
Healy, KS 67850

Iris Shrevei, an inhabitant of the moist regions of the prairie.

Eschscholzia californica

Chapter 4
The Chaparral Garden

The cobalt blue ceanothus blooms, the delicate pink manzanita flowers, and the drifts of California poppies glorify spring in northern California. In southern California the lavender sages, the majestic Matilija poppies, and the cheerful California red fuchsias give a dazzling show in summer. In New Mexico the brilliant yellow rabbit brush and alders contrast with the red soil to enliven fall. Throughout the Southwest native plants enrich our environment. Newcomers to this climate, unfamiliar with native plants and bent on duplicating an eastern garden, have often overlooked many of these beauties. If you want a spectacular flowerbed, instead of choosing the usual delphiniums, dahlias, and foxgloves that need continual staking, spraying, and watering, consider the pleasure and relative low maintenance of a flower border filled with lupines, velvet purple sages, ruby red penstemons, yellow fluffy buckwheat blooms, and California poppies. Not only are these natives much easier to maintain, most of them attract native hummingbirds and butterflies.

The American Southwest is an exciting place to garden. The native flora is extremely varied because there are more extremes of climate zones in the Southwest than in most of the rest of the world. It is not an unusual year when Mount Whitney registers 30 degrees below zero and Furnace Creek, less than one hundred miles away in Death Valley, registers 120 degrees six months later. In California some northern areas get more than one hundred inches of rain a year, while desert areas sometimes go a full year without any rain at all. In some places valuable moisture is available from fog or an occasional thunderstorm, but most plants native to the Southwest must adapt to limited water conditions, and adaptation over eons to the West's arid climates has filled this part of the world with literally thousands of drought-tolerant plant species. Thus, the gardener has many native plants to choose from that don't require constant watering and pampering.

The many climate zones, as well as proximity to the ocean and great variations in soils, have created a dramatic number of dominant plant communities in the Southwest. Those in the coastal areas supplement the winter rains with fog off the ocean. Plants from these areas will not grow well in dry inland gardens unless they have occasional summer watering. Redwood forests with wood sorrel and sword ferns; plants of the coastal strands—lupines, wild strawberries, and silk-tassel—all need some supplemental watering if grown in areas away from the coast. In sharp contrast to the fog-loving redwood forests are the deserts, where yuccas, pinon pines, and creosote bushes must be able to survive extreme summer temperatures with little moisture and, often, strongly alkaline soils, caliche (deposits of sand or clay impregnated with crystalline salts that are impenetrable to roots), and drying winds as well. Most of the desert plants not only don't need much water, they often can't tolerate it and sometimes have been labeled temperamental by gardeners who plant them near a lawn or feel sorry for them during midsummer and continually water them.

There are great variations in climate in the American Southwest, more than in many other areas of the world; therefore, you must be very aware of your microclimate when you choose native plants. When a plant is labeled *native*, the question has to be: native to where? A particular California native will not necessarily be appropriate to all parts of California, just as a particular Arizona native may not be native to all parts of Arizona. Consequently, a thorough investigation of your yard's climate is the first order of business when you want to select native plants.

In addition to considerations of climate, there are other factors that you must know about the plants of the Southwest when you are going to put in a garden of indigenous plants.

1. Because most residents in the Southwest are immigrants from rainier climates, typically we have chosen plants and garden styles that revolve around constant summer irrigation.

Therefore our garden practices and expectations are not always compatible with native plants. For example, lawn watering has killed many natives.

2. Most drought-tolerant plants can't tolerate much, if any, summer watering and generally need very fast drainage. (If watered too much, often they will appear to thrive the first few summers, only to die within two or three years.)

3. The seeds of a number of native plants need special treatment before they will germinate. In their native state some will not germinate until a fire has heated them or the acid in an animal's stomach has activated them. (There are ways of duplicating these processes, so don't be discouraged when seeds you have collected won't germinate.)

4. The majority of southwestern natives look their best in the winter and spring, and that does not always fit the expectations of gardeners from other parts of the country. The California buckeye, for instance, in order to avoid water loss, sheds its large fleshy leaves in midsummer. Many desert, or arid-climate, wildflowers have a short life cycle, blooming in the rainy spring and dying soon after. If you wish to counterbalance the winter- and spring-blooming natives, you can supplement them with compatible summer- and fall-blooming plants from other parts of the world.

5. Many of the southwestern native plants are very limited in their adaptability. They are quite fussy about the kind of soil, drainage, and watering they get.

6. A number of southwestern natives can adapt to many different soils and watering schedules and are useful for "fleshing out" your indigenous native garden or for using with your exotic plants. A few choices are: many of the native pines, baccharis, some of the ceanothus hybrids, toyon, redbud, monkey flower, and Douglas iris. (For many additional suggestions, see the publication of the Santa Barbara Botanic Garden that is described on page 64.)

7. Hillsides in various parts of the West are subject to erosion and slippage. Many of the native plants have very strong root systems and are useful to retain the soil. Select manzanita, Matilija poppy, buckwheat, ceanothus species, toyon, sumac, and oak species.

8. Many chaparral plants, including some that would do well in flower borders, such as sage, native grasses, and buckwheat, are quite flammable. Because fire is a hazard in much of the Southwest, plants like these should be used sparingly and should be combined with some of the fire-retarding plants such as ice plant, Capeweed, African daisy, toyon, and rosemary to offset fire danger. As a rule, using low flower borders like the one suggested, rather than many flammable trees near the house, makes your landscaping somewhat fire resistant.

9. Western native seeds and plants are in short supply in local nurseries. For a large selection, you will probably need to have your nursery order plants from one of the wholesale nurseries listed at the end of this chapter. If you are lucky, you will find a local retail nursery that specializes in native plants, and you can choose what you want there.

Southwestern native plants are versatile landscape plants that, when established in their native range, are easier to maintain, cost less to keep up, and use fewer resources than the traditional landscape plantings. Unfortunately many of these beautiful plants are used too infrequently. Still, they are "at home" in shrub borders and are useful as ground covers, shade trees, and vines. They make stunning, drought-tolerant flower borders.

Chaparral Flower Borders

The English perennial flower border has inspired many gardeners all over the world to duplicate this beautiful array of blooming plants. Unfortunately in arid climates gardeners have been frustrated because delphinium, astilbe, phlox, dahlia, foxglove, and many

Ceanothus, also known as California lilac, is covered with bright blue clusters of blossoms in the spring.

of the other perennials that are the backbone of those bouquet borders are hard to grow in arid conditions and need regular watering. Even when well watered, they never look as lush as they do in a cool moist climate.

Fortunately there are alternative flower borders for western gardens that can help assuage the craving for vast swaths of bright and varied flowers. Borders can be filled with flowering plants that love the heat and in most cases need little watering, plants that come primarily from the American Southwest and other arid climates of the world—the Mediterranean, South Africa, and Australia.

Because I favor native plants, I use them to form the backbone of my flower borders. There are bright yellow, orange, pink, purple, fire-engine red, and cobalt blue flowers, which attract native insects and hummingbirds. This rainbow of flowers is often set off by either gray or gray green foliage, and the combination is striking, making the borders quite distinctive. While it is possible to choose native species that bloom in late summer and fall, the majority of the western natives bloom in late winter, spring, and early summer. If you want to prolong the blooming season, select carefully for the late-blooming natives and flesh them out with a number of exotics that also bloom later. Not only are the resulting borders beautiful, they are versatile. They can be put in a small, sunny, sidewalk strip in the suburbs or on a hillside. They can be designed to be low maintenance, or they can be a lifetime hobby, constantly changing and challenging the gardener.

In order to accommodate the usual garden of exotic plants and natives from other parts of the West, most books for southwestern gardeners stress the great range of garden conditions that exist in people's gardens in order to acquaint gardeners with the changes in soil and watering they must make in their gardens. I, on the other hand, stress the differences in order to underline the importance of analyzing your site and climate, so you will appreciate how carefully you must match the plants to your conditions. The point is not to alter the conditions with soil amendments and watering schedules, but to fine-tune the right plants for the area.

I am not a purist; I am in full sympathy with the gardener who wants to have a showy garden all year round. Still, I think it is best to arrange the garden habitat around the indigenous habitat, its plants, and its animals. Then choose plants from other areas (exotics) that require similar growing conditions to enrich the planting. Don't impose a completely artificial habitat on the site, supplementing it with only an occasional native plant. To get ideas for your own chaparral garden, look at the coastal California shrub and flower garden filled with natives that is included in this chapter.

Planning and Preparation

Choose a sunny part of your yard. It can be down the side of the driveway, around the patio, on the back hillside, an area visible from the kitchen window, or up the front walk—anywhere that you will enjoy the show!

Measure the area and draw it to scale on paper. Lay sheets of tracing paper over the scale drawing, and make several designs. Use your imagination and play around with beds of different shapes. Also, experiment to see if a path through the garden is interesting. Add mounds and a boulder or two, or think about whether a fence across the back would make the area more interesting. For additional inspiration, look at pictures in garden books. Here are a few design hints.

1. Paths and fences near or in the bed will help unify the area and give it strong lines.

2. Most native plants are rather informal and look best with designs incorporating relaxed, curved, or freeform lines rather than straight lines, strong geometric forms, and clipped hedges.

3. Natural-looking materials such as wood and stone generally are the most pleasing visually.

4. Flat, level areas are often made more interesting with mounds or planter boxes.

5. Native flower borders work well with a number of inexpensive or recycled building materials, such as railroad ties, driftwood, used concrete paths and walls, recycled barn timbers, and telephone poles.

6. Unify the planting bed by choosing three or four species of plants that will predominate; otherwise, the design will be too jumbled.

7. Instead of using all colors, select three or four colors of flowers to unify the design, for example, red, orange, yellow, and white; or pink, purple, yellow, and blue; or red, yellow, and blue. Try to limit yourself as much as possible to the color combinations you choose.

After you have created a pleasing design on paper, determine your garden's soil conditions. Is the soil acidic or alkaline? sandy or clayey? Is the drainage good, or is the area boggy in the winter? What are the weather conditions? Determine the winter low and the summer high temperatures as well as the predominant wind direction. Is yours a sunny warm yard or a cool shady one? For more information, contact local experts: airports often have information on weather conditions, university extension people have soil information, and local nurseries and plant societies can help you analyze your soil conditions. The books listed at the end of this chapter also contain helpful information.

Once you know your climate, soil, and weather conditions, you can start looking for plants that will grow in your garden. Make a list of native and drought-tolerant flowering plants that you've found to be appropriate for your garden. Beside the name of each plant, write its height, flower color, and blooming season. Select the flower colors you would like. Choose plants of different heights, clustering the taller ones to the rear, the shorter ones in the front. Then select some plants that bloom at different times of the year so your garden will be interesting all year round. If you are using boulders or walls, cluster around them plants that have spiky foliage or flowers such as sage, Douglas iris, lupine, echium, red-hot-poker, and fortnight lily. If you are using retaining walls or planter boxes or are planting on a hillside, try plants that cascade, such as ivy geranium, prostrate rosemary, bougainvillea, African daisy, ice plant, lantana, and the native prostrate ceanothus, manzanita, and California fuchsia.

Planting the Drought-tolerant Garden

The best time to plant West Coast natives is in the fall before the rains come so that the roots can get well established before the long hot summer. Most drought-tolerant plants have strong, deep root systems. If possible, dig large planting holes. If gophers are a problem, surround the root ball with a basket made of chicken wire. Make sure that the basket protrudes above the ground three or four inches to prevent the gophers from crawling over the top. To prevent root-rot problems, plant the natives so that the crowns (where the bark meets the root tissue) are an inch or two above the soil

line, thus preventing water from covering that area for long periods of time. To conserve water and to add organic matter to the soil, mulch (cover the soil with two or three inches of organic matter) and water the plants well.

Most of the plants recommended in this chapter need biweekly watering the first two summers. Once the plants are established, they can survive the dry summer with only three or four waterings. Actually many of the natives can go through the whole summer with no supplemental watering; however, many gardeners prefer to water them a few times in the summer so they will be more lush. The most efficient and effective way to water is to use a drip irrigation system. (If you live in an area where the fire danger is high, consider, instead, installing an overhead watering system so that if a fire occurs, you could turn it on.)

Dr. Littauer planting in a wire basket for gopher control.

Maintaining the Drought-tolerant Border

Once established, usually in two years, the drought-tolerant border requires a minimum of maintenance. The bed will need annual pruning and fertilizing, weeding a few times a year, and an occasional watering. Pruning is particularly necessary for some of the rangy natives, such as dendromecon, sage, and Matilija poppy to keep them in bounds. Keep an eye out for an occasional gopher or pest problem. (Some of the plants recommended in this section, such as the fast-growing echium, lavender, and lantana and the ceanothus and sage are either short-lived or tend to get woody with age and need to be taken out and replaced in five or six years. All are fast growers, and replacements will fill in quickly.)

A Sample Garden

A beautiful model for a native, drought-tolerant flower border is the one I put together with Ernest and Deveda Littauer for their northern California yard. The Littauers' home is situated on a hillside and is surrounded by native chaparral. They wanted a design that included their patio hillside and the new deck area around the hot tub. The design for their yard had to take into account the Littauers' gardening style: They are avid gardeners but prefer propagating and putting in new plants, picking flowers, and puttering, to watering, weeding, spraying, mowing, and clipping. They love bright colors and unusual plants and were intent on using a number of native and drought-tolerant exotic plants in their garden.

The problems the Littauers have in their yard are similar to those of many hillside gardens on the West Coast; that is, fire danger, deer, and gophers. We reduced the fire danger by selecting fire-retarding plants and by eliminating those plants that are particularly combustible. We controlled the gophers primarily by planting most plants in chicken-wire baskets. We kept the deer problem to a minimum by choosing as many deer-resistant species as possible. Those included sage, African daisy, ice plant, rosemary, and echium. We also used the 'Dark Star' ceanothus, which is reputed to be somewhat deerproof.

To give coherence and strong lines to both hillside areas, we first created paths through the areas and sculptured some of the flat areas by adding mounds. The Littauers gave me carte blanche on plant choices, and, to unify the garden, I chose some of the Littauers' favorite colors: lavender, yellow, and blue. In addition, I used a number of plants with gray green foliage to help the garden merge into primarily gray green native chaparral. For the predominant vegetation I chose a number of blue ceanothus, sage, light pink ice plant, yellow dendromecon, many colors of penstemon, prostrate blue rosemary, and, for a fast-growing ground cover, yellow Capeweed. To give more summer and fall bloom, I added lavender echium, white fortnight lily, pink New Zealand tea, and, given my penchant for edible plants, a beautiful red-flowered pomegranate.

Responding with enthusiasm to the delightful spectrum of native plants, the Littauers soon started propagating and planting many more natives, a list of which follows. The Littauers' experience yielded a few words of advice.

1. The couple visited a nursery expressly devoted to native plants and received advice as well as getting a large selection of plants.

2. They were observant gardeners and noticed that the Matilija poppy was starting to become invasive, so they took it out.

3. They started to grow many of the natives from seed so that they would have a larger selection. (Ernest stresses strongly that it is important to start your native seeds in a sterile medium such as perlite so that they don't develop fungus problems.)

4. Ernest admonishes you not to feel sorry for and water the very drought tolerant plants when they start to look parched in the summer.

5. As beginning native gardeners, they found the book *California Native Trees and Shrubs* invaluable.

6. The Littauers have a windy yard and found that a number of their plants blew over, particularly when gophers had been eating the roots. They recommend heavily pruning the taller plants that are prone to wind damage.

7. They also experienced the frustration of an exotic plant "gone crazy"—a previously planted Scotch broom became a nuisance—it spread too freely—and needed to be eradicated.

Native Plants for a Drought-tolerant Garden

Buckwheat, *Eriogonum* species, chartreuse, white, brown

Bush poppy, *Dendromecon rigida,* yellow

California fuchsia, *Zauschneria californica,* red

California lilac, *Ceanothus* species, blue, white

California poppy, *Eschscholzia californica,* orange, yellow

Douglas iris, *Iris Douglasiana,* white, purple

Evening primrose, *Oenothera Hookeri,* yellow

Fremontodendron, *Fremontodendron californicum,* yellow

Island bush snapdragon, *Galvezia speciosa,* red

Lupine, *Lupinus arboreus,* purple, yellow, white

Manzanita, *Arctostaphylos* species, pink

Monkey flower, *Mimulus* species, yellow, orange

Penstemon, *Penstemon cordifolius,* red, yellow

Redbud, *Cercis occidentalis,* magenta

Sage, *Salvia* species, purple, red, lavender

Sugarbush, *Rhus ovata,* red, cream

Toyon, *Heteromeles arbutifolia,* white, red berries

Tree anemone, *Carpenteria californica,* white

Penstemon

Nonnative, Drought-tolerant Flowering Plants

The following nonnatives combine well with California natives. They require little water and will grow in many climate zones in the West. Choose those that will grow well in your area. These perennials can be supplemented with spring-blooming wildflowers and bulbs.

African daisy, *Arctotis* species, orange, yellow
    and *Osteospermum fruticosum,* purple, white
Aloe, *Aloe* species, red, yellow
Bougainvillea, *Bougainvillea* species, rose,
    red, orange, purple
Cape honeysuckle, *Tecomaria capensis,*
    orange
Capeweed, *Arctotheca calendula,* yellow
Echium, *Echium* species, purple
Fortnight lily, *Dietes vegeta,* white
Geranium, *Pelargonium* species, red, orange,
    lavender, pink
Grevillea, *Grevillea* species (low-growing
    types), red, pink
Iris, *Iris* species (bearded types), older varieties
    are more drought tolerant
Lantana, *Lantana* species, yellow, pink, laven-
    der, white, red, salmon
Lavender, *Lavandula* species, lavender
Natal plum, *Carissa* species, white
New Zealand tea, *Leptospermum* species,
    pink, rose
Oleander, *Nerium Oleander* (dwarf types),
    salmon, pink
Pineapple guava, *Feijoa Sellowiana,* reddish
Plumbago, *Plumbago auriculata,* blue
Pomegranate, *Punica Granatum,* red
Red-hot-poker, *Kniphofia Uvaria,* red, yellow,
    white
Rock rose, *Cistus* species, white, pink
Rosemary, *Rosmarinus* species, blue
Sedum, *Sedum* species, white, pink, yellow
Senecio, *Senecio Greyi,* yellow
Statice (sea lavender), *Limonium Perezii,*
    lavender

Scrub oak

The layout of this chaparral garden emphasizes blooming plants. The Littauers' chaparral garden is ablaze with blue ceanothus, yellow Capeweed and dendromecon, pink New Zealand tea, and white African daisies. It can be viewed from both the deck and the house. To give the garden form as well as color, retaining walls and a curving path were added.

1. African daisies
2. New Zealand tea
3. Capeweed
4. Ceanothus 'Ray Hartman'
5. Rock rose
6. Ceanothus 'Dark Star'
7. Mexican bush sage
8. Dendromecon
9. Pomegranate
10. Lemon
11. Lime
12. Lion's-tail sage
13. Pink ice plant
14. Bougainvillea
15. Fremontodendron
16. Purple sage
17. Penstemon
18. Echium
19. Ceanothus 'Snow Ball'
20. Redbud
21. Rosemary
22. Fortnight lily
23. Lavender

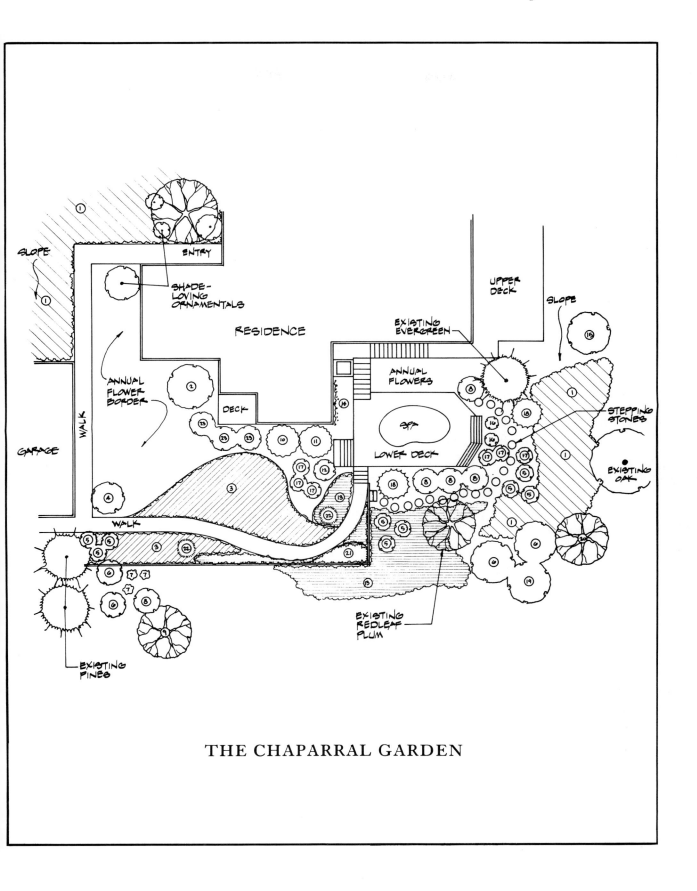

THE CHAPARRAL GARDEN

Sources of Information

Books

Lenz, Lee W., and Dourley, John. *California Native Trees and Shrubs for Garden and Environmental Use in Southern California and Adjacent Areas*. Claremont, Calif.: Rancho Santa Ana Botanic Garden, 1981. This book is excellent for the gardener who is just beginning to use native plants.

Ortho Books, Chevron Chemical Company editorial staff. *All About Perennials*. San Francisco: Ortho Books, 1981. This book is primarily about water-loving nonnative plants; however, it has valuable information about how to work with perennial flower borders and flower color.

Ortho Books, Chevron Chemical Company editorial staff. *The World of Cactuses and Succulents*. San Francisco: Ortho Books, 1977. How to grow, select, and maintain cactuses and succulents.

Perry, Bob. *Trees and Shrubs for Dry California Landscapes*. San Dimas, Calif.: Land Design Publishing, 1981. Valuable information about drought-tolerant plants; color prints.

Santa Barbara Botanic Garden. *Native Plants for Southern California Gardens*. No. 12. Santa Barbara: Santa Barbara Botanic Garden, 1969. Detailed information on California native plants and the growing conditions they prefer.

Saratoga Horticultural Foundation. *Selected California Native Plants with Commercial Sources*. 3rd ed. Saratoga, Calif.: Saratoga Horticultural Foundation, 1983. This book is particularly helpful in finding sources for the native plants you want.

Smith, Ken. *Western Home Landscaping*. Tucson, Ariz.: H.P. Books, 1978. A helpful book for home landscapers. It has quite a bit of information on drought-tolerant plants and how to put in a drip irrigation system.

Sunset Books editorial staff. *New Western Garden Book*. Menlo Park, Calif.: Lane Publishing Co., 1979. This book is a must for all western gardeners; it's considered the bible of West Coast gardening.

Additional information on native and drought-tolerant plants is available from the California State Water Resources Board and from many local water districts.

Demonstration Gardens

Rancho Santa Ana Botanic Garden
1500 North College Avenue
Claremont, CA 91711

Regional Parks Botanic Garden
Tilden Regional Park
Berkeley, CA 94708

Santa Barbara Botanic Garden
1212 Mission Canyon Road
Santa Barbara, CA 93105

Nurseries

Ask your local nursery to order from the following wholesale sources.

For northern California:

Saratoga Horticultural Foundation
20605 Verde Vista Lane
Saratoga, CA 95070

For midcoast and southern California:

Native Sons
379 West El Campo Road
Arroyo Grande, CA 93420

Tree of Life Nursery
P.O. Box 736
San Juan Capistrano, CA 92693

You can order seeds by mail from:

Clyde Robin Seed Company
P.O. Box 2366
Castro Valley, CA 94546

Consumer Note

Two hints on obtaining southwestern natives are: (1) many of the drought-tolerant natives have long taproots and don't do well in nursery containers; buy them as small as possible, or start them in place from seed; and (2) get to know and frequent local native plant nurseries, and join your native plant society; they will be your best sources of information and plants.

Yucca species

PART TWO
ARK GARDENS

Recreating and preserving ecosystems are effective ways of enabling nature to preserve itself, but setting up such environments often results in fairly stable, low-maintenance yards that for some people just don't satisfy the need to roll up the sleeves and *garden*. In seeking an outlet for an abundance of creative energy, both active gardeners and frustrated conservationists might consider adopting this chapter's guiding concept: the garden as ark, a la Noah himself. The idea here is to seek out and save plant species—both wild and domestic—that are threatened with extinction. Raise them in a garden designed especially to allow them to thrive, safe from the rigors of an advancing civilization seemingly bent on stamping them out. The challenge and excitement of rescuing and growing a rare orchid or caring for an endangered rose that was once grown in ancient Rome give zest to gardening.

When we think of Noah's Ark, we picture lions, tigers, and giraffes, not daffodils, lady's-slippers, and sacks of seeds. People think in terms of saving animals, not plants; and, hence, modern Noahs tend to be more interested in saving whales and baby seals than prairie bunch grasses and tropical orchids.

What good does it do, though, to save the giant panda and not its bamboo habitat? I don't dispute the necessity of saving animals, but if we fail to preserve plants and their ecosystems, the animals that depend on those plants will disappear no matter what.

Sometimes I feel like the child in *The Emperor's New Clothes*. Nearly every column, book, or conference on gardening is filled with news of the latest ruffled petunia or new rose color. "Look," they say, "the world is filled with new and better plants." I want to get up on a rooftop and shout, "Hold it! What about the species we're losing?" For every new petunia or begonia we create each week, we allow three species of plants in the wild to become extinct; and we doom to the scrap heap numerous "out-of-fashion" domestic plants. How can so many plant lovers be so blind? Ninety percent of the material written about plants in this country is concerned with the newest cultivated plants; it ignores the historical domestic species and the grim plight of the ever-more-vulnerable wild species. We gardeners must get involved in preserving plants. Let's hear it for the endangered *plant* species of the world!

Why should we bother to save ecosystems and rare and heritage plants? Some cite philosophical reasons, saying that such organisms and environments have as much right to existence on earth as we do. Others want to preserve them because it is fun to work with these living pieces of history. But the practical reasons should convince us of the necessity for conservation. Like the panda, *we* can't survive without plants. While it appears that this country runs on Big Macs, the real fuel is the ten pounds of hay per pound of body weight consumed by the cattle from which our Big Macs are made. Moreover, if animals disappeared from this planet, we would still eat well. As it is, plants provide food, clothing, and shelter for the majority of the people on earth. In addition to providing basic human needs, plants enrich our lives by giving us healing medicines, shade on sweltering summer days, and even the cotton for our jeans.

Herbal Medicine

Take two pieces of willow bark and call me in the morning. Because our medicines come in bottles and have unfamiliar names, few of us are aware that many of them have been derived from plants. Digitalis, which regulates the heartbeat, comes from foxglove; ipecac, which induces vomiting and is helpful in cases where poison has been ingested, comes from the roots of the cephaelis plant; and quinine, which controls malaria, comes from cinchona trees. Even the precursor to good old aspirin was first discovered in a plant: willow bark. Less well known is the fact that many of the so-called wonder drugs discovered between 1930 and 1960 were of vegetative origin: antibiotics come from molds, and reserpine comes from Indian snake root. Oral contraceptives and cortisone resulted from research done on the Mexican yam. It seems ironic, but just as medical botany is taking off, well equipped with spectrographs, electron microscopes, and computers to analyze and take advantage of newly discovered plants, many ecosystems and their plants are slipping away.

In areas other than medical botany, plant life is being explored as an important resource. In Israel, for example, certain plants are being bred to serve as indicators of pollution levels. Elsewhere, a certain wild cucumber has been discovered that can temporarily acidify human seminal fluid, thus offering a contraceptive method that could revolutionize birth control. And in the new field of genetic engineering, though the actuality is years away, scientists are developing the potential to implant a gene from a bean plant into a tomato plant to make the tomato plant capable of fixing nitrogen in the soil the way the bean plant does. Such a tomato would not need as much nitrogen fertilizer as our contemporary varieties do. In theory, then, eventually we will be able to create almost any kind of plant we want, feature by feature, so long as we maintain a large enough gene pool to draw from.

Nearly 200 species of wild plants are lost every year, and the rate of loss is accelerating. The shocking truth is that biologists estimate that by the year 2000, 25 percent, or 40,000 species, of higher plants will be extinct. Compare that estimate with the historical figures: A mere 200 species have been lost over the last 500 years.

What can we do? As I stated in Part One, saving endangered plant species begins with preserving ecosystems. And while it is of value to keep endangered species alive by growing them in an alien habitat, once plants are taken out of their natural habitats and domesticated, they, like animals, change subtly over generations, adapting to their new environments. In addition, many species, although they stay alive for a number of years, fail to reproduce in an altered environment, so only their fleeting presence is gained. In Part Two, based on the assumption that you have maintained the natural ecosystem in at least a portion of your yard, I give detailed information on active conservation measures that are meant both to satisfy your passion for gardening and to preserve nature's diversity.

What the Master Gardener Can Do

If you are one of our nation's true plant mavens, you may be skilled enough to raise and propagate, in an approximation of their original habitats, some of the endangered orchids, cactuses, succulents, or other wild species. While this is not the optimum situation, at least it may keep them alive until a suitable habitat for them can be found. In addition, some rare plants that propagate easily can be maintained in the garden as a means of educating the public about the need to conserve rare plants. (Experienced gardeners should contact Dr. Rolf Martin, Department of Chemistry, Brooklyn College, Brooklyn, NY 11210, to learn about the program of the Rare and Endangered Native Plant Exchange.) Furthermore, keeping these endangered plants alive may help future breeding programs or provide seeds for wild areas.

Adele Dawson in Vermont takes an active part in saving native plants such as this bottle gentian that she saved from the snowplow's blade. Keep an eye out for possible development areas and become involved in saving plants that would otherwise be destroyed.

Gardens with a Purpose

Domestic plants as well as wild ones need an ark. Save seeds from open-pollinated (non-hybrid) vegetables and fill your yard with endangered domestic plants, both ornamental and edible. The gardens described in Part Two —the heirloom vegetable garden, the wildlife garden, the heritage rose garden, and the orchid garden—incorporate these principles with dazzling effects.

When we think of an endangered plant species, we almost always envision a beleaguered plant out in the wild. But wild plants are not the only ones endangered. More and more botanists are becoming aware that our valuable domestic gene pool is being depleted at an ever-accelerating rate.

By *gene pool* I mean the rich heritage of flowers and edibles that people have been cultivating for centuries. Some of these plants have origins as far back as ancient Greece and Rome. Even some of the plants that our great-great-grandparents grew one hundred years ago were quite different from those that we have in our gardens today. In fact, the gardens of our great-great-grandparents had many flowers and vegetables we may never have seen: red celery, 'Howling Mob' corn, 'Maiden's Blush' roses, 'Dwarf-Giant' tomato, 'Lazy Wife's' beans, and thousands more.

What has happened to those plant species? Many simply dropped out of favor. Gardening is as susceptible to the whims of fashion as any other endeavor in our society. During the last ten to twenty years, for example, fragrant roses were out of favor and large double petunias were in. Now it looks as if fragrant roses are coming back into vogue. Also back with us are some of the old-fashioned single petunias and some of the more subtle marigolds and zinnias. Certainly there are many varieties to choose from, particularly when it comes to ornamental plants. Over the hundreds of years that people have been cultivating plants, there have been,

for example, between 17,000 and 18,000 varieties of daffodils. Not all of the thousands of varieties are of value, but many of the old-timers that have disappeared would be cherished today. Some have unusual forms; many were very fragrant; still others grew with little water. Sadly, however, when these plants go out of favor, within a generation or two they often disappear altogether—another example of our "throw-away" culture.

The sight of some of Great-Aunt Polly's and Great-Uncle Jack's fruits and vegetables would probably surprise you. Instead of a 'Granny Smith' apple tree or 'Thompson Seedless' grapes, they may have had a 'Red Astrachan' or a 'Baldwin' apple tree or 'Muscat of Alexandria' grapes. And they may have grown some particularly tasty, but odd-colored, vegetables, such as yellow beets and tomatoes, purple broccoli and cauliflower, and blue corn and potatoes. Besides varieties unfamiliar to contemporary gardeners, they may have grown types of edibles that are out of favor now; for instance, there were gooseberries, quince, Good King Henry (a spinachlike vegetable), and rampion (a white edible tuber).

Corporations and the Seed Business

Fashion and taste aren't the only reasons your edible garden differs from those of your ancestors. Our evolving understanding of breeding techniques has resulted in great improvements in disease resistance and plant adaptability and vigor. Unfortunately for home gardeners, many of the improvements developed by breeders have been aimed at the needs of the commercial grower. Years ago vegetable plants acclimated to people's own gardens and tastes because year after year gardeners collected the seeds from their best plants, those that grew best in their miniclimates and the ones whose taste they preferred. Nowadays many of the available varieties are determined

by the corporations that control the seed industry. An analogy with the clothing industry comes to my mind: Today most of us have sacrificed the style and fit of personally tailored clothes for the convenience and low cost of garments off the rack.

While some wonderful new hybrid vegetables and fruits (that is, plants created through selected crossbreeding) have been made available for home gardeners, it's their biggest customer, the farmer, whose interests increasingly dominate seed-breeding. The seed companies, to help the farmer, have bred for yield and disease resistance. While those characteristics have indisputably benefited the home grower, other characteristics; namely, uniformity in size, ability to withstand machine picking and sorting, uniform ripening, and the ability to ripen after harvest, are not in the interests of home gardeners but have been foisted upon them.

Nevertheless, those modern miracles, the cardboard tomato, the tasteless strawberry, and the juiceless peach—always available, handsome to look at, and a waste of the effort it takes to chew, much less grow—are a reality. With "progress" we are losing the delicious varieties of yesteryear.

Seed Saving

What can be done before it's too late? The solution is to grow many of the open-pollinated varieties of vegetables and to save seeds—so obvious and simple a solution to the problem that it might embarrass you, as it did me when I first started doing it. Turn now to the detailed description of a simple-to-create heirloom vegetable garden, in the following chapter, where you will find a thorough discussion of the time-honored practice of saving seeds.

PLANT RUSTLING

Rustled plants are those that are taken illegally from the wild. Plant rustlers go out into wild areas and dig up rare plants as well as some that are on the endangered species list, often illegally taking plants from private lands or national parks. The most commonly rustled plants are native orchids and cactuses. Plants from both of these families are slow growing, sometimes taking as long as five to ten years to be of salable size. Some of these plants are bought on impulse by the homeowner who just wants a few inexpensive house plants; still others are bought by collectors of rare plants. Collectors often don't realize the pressure they put on endangered plants in the wild and on the legitimate nursery people who propagate the rare plants only to compete with rustlers who sometimes sell the black-market plants out of the back of their trucks. Plant rustlers have no greenhouses to heat, no plants to water, and no expensive endangered-plant inspection permits to buy.

Ironically, while endangered-plant legislation was created to protect plants, according to the people at Grigsby's Cactus Nursery and other conscientious growers, the Endangered Species Act sometime does more harm than good. For instance, buying and selling of endangered species are controlled, and inspections are made and paid for when plants are sold across state lines. These controls increase the cost of growing plants legitimately and make the low prices charged by the black-market rustlers even more attractive. If the public stops buying from plant rustlers, fewer endangered plants will be taken illegally from the wild and legitimate growers will be encouraged to grow them in abundance.

Faith Campbell, a member of the Natural Resources Defense Council, gives the following guidelines for avoiding rustled plants. Be very cautious when buying any unusual plants. If the price seems too good to be true, it probably is. Buy only from established nurseries; never buy from roadside stands or trucks. Ask whether the plants were propagated. Notice whether the dealer has many plants of the same size and species. Notice whether cactuses and succulents look fresh, green, and symmetrical or "beat up," scarred, and skewed in shape. Most propagated cactuses will be small, symmetrical, and unscarred. Ask about care of the plants; if the seller can't tell you, he probably didn't propagate them.

There are a few plants to be particularly careful about because they are threatened by extinction. They are living-rock cactus, *Ariocarpus agavoides;* Aztec cactus, *Aztekium Ritteri;* artichoke cactus, *Obregonia Denegrii;* Amalia orchid, *Laelia jongheana;* blue vanda orchid, *Vanda coerulea;* fire orchid, *Renanthera Imschootiana;* green pitcher plant, *Sarracenia oreophila;* mountain sweet pitcher plant, *Sarracenia Jonesii;* giant pitcher plant, *Nepenthes rajah;* ghostman, *Pachypodium namaquanum;* spiral aloe, *Aloe polyphylla;* and broadleaf cycad, *Encephalartos latifrons.*

For a list of nurseries that propagate most, if not all, of their own native plants, write to The New England Wild Flower Society, Garden in the Woods, Hemenway Road, Framingham, MA 01701. The catalog is $1.50.

Cactuses and succulents that have been propagated in a
nursery usually look healthier and more uniform than those
that have been dug up (illegally, no doubt) in the wild. When
looking for unusual native plants, frequent reputable nurseries
such as Grigsby's, where a number of endangered species are
propagated.

Chapter 5

The Heirloom Vegetable Garden

Just as civilization has saved "Aida," the Mona Lisa, and *Macbeth* for future generations, so should we save seeds of old-time vegetables and grafting material of heirloom fruit trees, says Carolyn Jabs in her book *The Heirloom Gardener*. They represent valuable achievements made by generations of gardeners and give a large range of choices to our descendants. Annual vegetable varieties are gossamer entities. Unlike a concerto that might be out of favor for a few years but is preserved because it is written on a sheet of paper, a carrot that has been grown for centuries can disappear in a year or two if no one grows it.

Growing an heirloom vegetable garden is an exciting variation on the usual array of current varieties such as 'Yolo Wonder' peppers, 'Silver Queen' corn, and 'Early Girl' tomatoes. It's stimulating to try the old-time yellow tomatoes, purple broccoli, and cylindrical potatoes, not to mention the feeling of kinship you'll have

with previous generations while you shell the same kind of beans your great-grandmother might have shelled.

Some of these old varieties have traits that make them valuable eating in their own right, while others may be good only for future breeding stock. The effect of acid rain, carbon monoxide, and salty irrigation water on plants, for example, could not have been predicted one hundred years ago. Some of the old varieties will grow well with less nitrogen or water; others are more salt tolerant. There will be many problems in the future that we can't foresee; therefore, it makes sense to keep as many plant-gene options as possible open for future generations.

How serious is the problem of annual vegetable variety erosion? Very! Thousands of varieties have already been lost. Kent Whealy, founder of Seed Savers Exchange, figures that only 20 percent of the pea varieties once in cultivation are still available. In the early 1900s a scientist compiled a list of 8,000 varieties of apples, and in 1981 the USDA could find only 1,000 varieties.

A great loss of varieties happened in the early part of this century when seed saving was discouraged and hybrid seeds were introduced. (In plant breeding, hybridizers cross specially selected strains and produce a second generation with desired characteristics.) Hybrid vegetables and grains have made American farms the most productive in the world, but, as with everything else in life, there have been trade-offs. Home gardeners have benefited from hybrids that are more disease resistant, more vigorous and higher yielding, but the cost has been high. Not collecting seeds means buying seeds and being dependent on seed companies, which means fewer options for home growing.

The erosion of home varieties is starting to snowball. The new wave of losses is a result of a growing national trend—the buying up and consolidation of many small seed companies by multinational corporations. The major seed companies, once owned by seedsmen, are now owned and run by business people. For example, ITT now owns Burpee; Monsanto owns Farmer's Hybrid; the Swiss corporation Sandoz owns Northrup-King; and Purex owns Ferry-Morse. Now the accountants as strongly as the seed people influence what is grown. And because farmers buy the great majority of seeds in this country, varieties of vegetables that are tailored for agriculture—extra-firm for shipping, simultaneous ripening of the whole crop—are now stressed. As a consequence, countless home varieties are being dropped.

You can help. You can save some of your own seeds. You can share them with others. You can join a seed-saving organization and grow some of the rarer varieties. Even some of the old woody carrot varieties and mealy potatoes have value, because some are particularly disease resistant. You can help also by spreading the word. Most of the media is flooded with the latest information on the newest hybrid. These hybrids are usually great, but we have relied too much on them, and an adjustment period is needed.

The panda and the snow leopard are endangered, and often we can do nothing more than send a check to a conservation organization or a letter to a senator. Saving heirloom seeds, however, has a direct impact on the problem. In addition, growing heirloom varieties is interesting; it's a great way to get a sense of history. Perhaps it will bring back a childhood memory and save you some money. You may very well discover that 'Howling Mob' corn and 'Purple' beans are the tastiest vegetables you have ever eaten.

Planning and Preparation

Because of the unpredictability of a first-time heirloom vegetable garden (that is, not knowing how well each variety will do in your garden and not knowing how well you will like each variety), you should not plan it as your only vegetable garden. Rather, it can be an exciting addition to some of your tried-and-true favorites.

To start your heirloom garden, you must obtain the seeds, thus, your introduction to seed saving. There are a number of ways to obtain seeds of heirloom species. The best way is to talk with some of your neighbors to find out if they have any varieties to share with you. If you don't come up with anything, contact Seed Savers Exchange or one of the other seed-saving organizations, or buy your seeds from one of the new seed companies that cater to heirloom growers. (See the lists of organizations and seed companies at the end of this chapter.)

Making your seed selections will take some research. There is much more variability with some of the old-time varieties than with hybrids in adaptability, viability, and yield. Some varieties taste better; some taste worse than what you're used to; some are just different. Some of the old string-bean varieties, for example, are particularly tasty, but each bean has a string down the side that is too tough to eat and must be pulled off; hence, the name *string* bean, right? You may like the taste but not the stringing.

Another characteristic of many of the old varieties is that they keep well. Before refrigeration it was critical that vegetables keep for long periods of time without rotting. Consequently, many of the old turnip, carrot, beet, and cabbage varieties can be stored very well in a root cellar. Another factor to consider when growing heirlooms is that while many of the varieties are disease resistant, others are particularly prone to certain diseases, and others have a very limited optimum-growth environmental range.

The limitations of some of the old varieties are what helped to make hybrids as popular today as they are. Hybrids offer adaptability, yield, and disease resistance. Remember, though, that one of the goals of growing heirloom plants is to make sure that we have the necessary starting points for future hybridization.

Begin by choosing six to eight varieties. The easiest families to start with are the legumes—beans and peas—and the solanaceae—tomatoes, peppers, and eggplants. Order a catalog from one of the recommended seed companies. Stick to open-pollinated varieties, no hybrids; the reasons will become clear as you read on.

You may want to order an heirloom vegetable kit from either Seeds Blum (the address is given at the end of this chapter), which carries a seed-saver's kit that includes nine varieties of vegetables, many of which are listed below, or from Roger A. Kline, Department of Vegetable Crops, Plant Science Building, Ithaca, NY 14853. Kline offers both large and small kits. The largest has twenty-two varieties, more than enough for a "demon" heirloom gardener. Some of the varieties in the

Carl Barnes of Oklahoma has been collecting and growing heirloom varieties of corn since 1946. His dedication to saving old corn varieties includes hand-pollinating the varieties he grows in order to prevent cross-pollination. He has been instrumental in organizing a group called CORNS.

large kit are 'Alaska' pea, 'Black Mexican' corn, 'Drumhead Savoy' cabbage, 'Jacob's Cattle' bean, 'Lady Finger' potato, 'Long Season' beet, 'Ponderosa' tomato, 'Purple-top Strap-leaf' turnip, 'Red Wethersfield' onion, and 'White Bush Scallop' squash. All kits include detailed seed-saving information.

Or you may want to choose from the lists that Jan Blum, owner of one of the new seed companies that is devoted to heirloom seeds, has put together. She has chosen heirloom vegetable varieties that she thinks are valuable and superior. The seeds are available from a number of the seed companies that carry heirloom seeds (an annotated list of those companies appears at the end of this chapter). If you are a beginning heirloom gardener and seed saver, Blum recommends that you start with the following varieties: 'Black Valentine' bean, 'Blue Coco' bean, 'Blue Pod' pea, 'Jacob's Cattle' bean, 'May King' lettuce, 'Oakleaf' lettuce, 'Persimmon' tomato, 'Ruby King' pepper, 'Super Italian' paste tomato, 'Tall Telephone' pea, and 'Wren's Egg' bean.

For experienced gardeners and seed savers, she recommends the following varieties because they offer more of a challenge: 'Dutch White Runner' bean, 'Early Scarlet Horn' carrot, 'French Breakfast' radish, Good King Henry (a type of green), purple broccoli, red celery, sea kale, 'Shoepeg' corn, and 'Windermoor Wonder' cucumber. Some of the varieties, such as the celery and the broccoli, are more challenging because they are hard to grow, but most of the items on the list are there simply because they need hand-pollinating or because the seed-saving process is more complex than for those on the beginner's list.

A Prototype Heirloom Vegetable Garden

A good way to start your seed-saving adventure is to use the accompanying garden as a guide. Choose a part of your yard that receives at least six hours of sun each day. The layout of this garden is north to south, because you don't want taller plants such as corn and pole beans to shade the shorter vegetables. I have chosen a summer heirloom garden to start because most of the vegetables are easy to grow. If you have questions, read the information in *Vegetables: How to Select, Grow, and Enjoy* by Derek Fell. The heirloom varieties are grown the same way that modern vegetables are. Take note of the layout; not only is it important to have taller vegetables at the back, but when you are seed saving, you must try to isolate the plants that may cross-pollinate. Therefore, the different bean varieties have been separated by rows of other vegetables.

You can plant heirloom varieties of corn and cucumbers in your garden if you can isolate them; however, if you or your neighbors are growing other varieties of cucumbers or corn within 300 feet, you cannot save the seeds because the pollen from the other varieties may be carried to your heirloom plants, pollinating them and changing the next generation of the heirloom varieties.

Saving Seeds

People stopped regularly saving seeds early in this century when hybrid seeds—seeds produced by selectively bred plants—were introduced. Because hybrid seeds do not come true from seed—that is, succeeding generations are not like the parent plant—saving seeds was no longer worthwhile. Hybrid seeds virtually guaranteed the seed companies that their customers would return year after year. Over the last sixty or seventy years the American public has been so conditioned to buy seeds for the latest hybrids that a generation or two of gardeners has not learned how to save seeds from favorite plants.

As I said earlier, I never even thought about saving my own seeds when I started vegetable gardening. Seeds, in my experience, came in beautiful packages, not from my plants. I have just recently begun to learn about seed saving and have been amazed at how simple and satisfying it is. I keep a few 'Dutch White Runner' beans each year for the next year's crop. When they are completely dry, I freeze them for a day to kill any weevil eggs that may be in them, and label them—that's all there is to it. Once I went through the process, I felt like a chump for having faithfully sent off to Maine every spring for a new package of 'Dutch White Runner' beans—an open-pollinated variety that I could have saved easily myself.

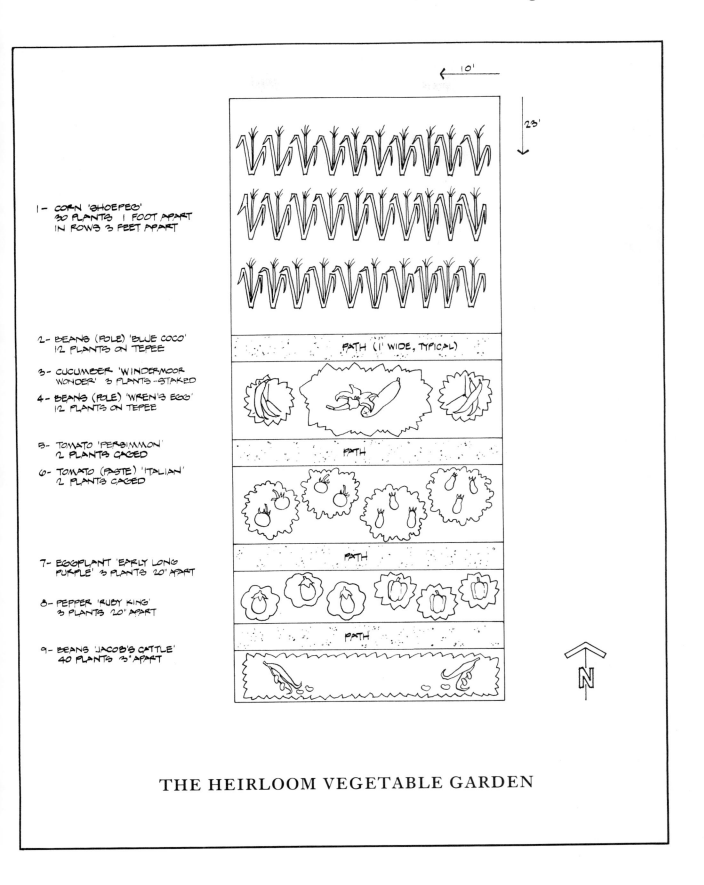

1– CORN 'SHOEPEG'
30 PLANTS 1 FOOT APART
IN ROWS 3 FEET APART

2– BEANS (POLE) 'BLUE COCO'
12 PLANTS ON TEPEE

3– CUCUMBER 'WINDERMOOR
WONDER' 3 PLANTS –STAKED

4– BEANS (POLE) 'WREN'S EGG'
12 PLANTS ON TEPEE

5– TOMATO 'PERSIMMON'
2 PLANTS CAGED

6– TOMATO (PASTE) 'ITALIAN'
2 PLANTS CAGED

7– EGGPLANT 'EARLY LONG
PURPLE' 3 PLANTS 20" APART

8– PEPPER 'RUBY KING'
3 PLANTS 20" APART

9– BEANS 'JACOB'S CATTLE'
40 PLANTS 3" APART

THE HEIRLOOM VEGETABLE GARDEN

I want to begin this explanation on how to save seeds with a review of the birds-and-bees information we think we know all about, until we are called upon to explain it. The reproduction of seed plants involves the transference of pollen, which contains the sperm cells produced by the male flower part, the stamen, to the stigma, which contains the ovary, the female organ. This transfer process is called *pollination*. Once a plant has been pollinated, seeds form. If the pollen from a flower fertilizes the ovary of the same flower, the process is called *self-pollination*. To self-pollinate, a flower must have both stamen and stigma; such a flower is called a *perfect* flower. Beans and peas have perfect flowers and are usually self-pollinated. When there is a transference of pollen, either between flowers on the same plant or between flowers on different plants, the process is called *cross-pollination*. In that case, pollen is carried from flower to flower either by an insect or by the wind. Corn, squash, broccoli, and beets are cross-pollinated.

In seed saving your aim is to preserve existing varieties unaltered. To do so, it is necessary to avoid cross-pollination of the plant you intend to preserve. Say, for example, that you have a banana squash plant situated next to a zucchini plant. Along comes a bee that visits a male flower on the banana squash plant then flies to a female flower on the zucchini plant, transferring pollen from banana squash to zucchini—cross-pollinating the zucchini. If you planted the seeds from the pollinated zucchini the next year, the result would be a cross between the two plants. Sometimes the cross produces a good offspring, and that's one way we get new varieties. Usually, you'll just get a weird squash. I remember once letting some squash plants mature that had sprouted in the compost pile. I got a cross between a striped summer ball squash and an acorn squash: a striped, tough-skinned, stringy summer squash.

You can see that when you intend to save the seeds of your plants in order to preserve varieties over the generations, you must always take steps to prevent cross-pollination. With plants such as beans, which have perfect flowers and usually pollinate themselves before they open, cross-pollination is seldom a problem. Others, such as plants in the squash and cucumber family, cross-pollinate readily and must be planted in isolation to ensure that the variety will remain pure.

There are a number of ways to isolate plants. First, you can plant only one variety of each type of vegetable, since cross-pollination does not occur between different genera. Second, you can plant potential cross-pollinators far from each other. Some varieties need only one hundred feet between them; others require half a mile. This is where your research—getting information from books on the subject or from nurseries that specialize in open-pollinated varieties—pays off. Finally, you can use a physical barrier: a number of rows of tall corn between the species, or plant the species on either side of an existing building.

I have mentioned that saving the seeds of hybrids is wasted energy, since hybrid seeds don't reproduce true. A hybrid is analogous to a mule. You get a mule by crossing a horse with a donkey; that is, you cross closely related species to create a new entity. That is also how a hybrid is created. The second generation, the mule, however, is sterile (not *all* hybrids are sterile). When you want to produce another mule, you must again cross a horse and a donkey; mules don't beget mules. In plant breeding, hybridists cross specially selected strains to produce a generation that possesses desired characteristics as well as what is called *hybrid vigor* (unusually strong or productive plants). Because you don't know which parents were crossed to create your hybrid plant (it's all a trade secret), you cannot produce the offspring. When you save seeds, then, you have to know which are pure, or open-pollinated, varieties and which are hybrids. Those that are open-pollinated are the only ones you can reproduce consistently. To prevent confusion, seed nurseries label the hybrids. That information is indicated in the catalog and on the seed packet. You may notice the designation "F1 hybrid"—that is simply a form of hybrid.

In addition to knowing about pollination and hybrids, you must know the life cycles of the plants you are dealing with. While the life cycles of most of our vegetables are annual (maturing in one season), many are biennial, which means that they take two seasons to reproduce. Some popular biennials are beets, carrots, parsley, and chard; and these will not produce seeds the first growing season.

If you are a novice seed saver, you will benefit from reading the pamphlet *Growing Garden Seeds* by Robert Johnston, Jr. It is available from Johnny's Selected Seeds, Albion, ME 04910, for $2.50. For a complete discussion of seed saving, with lists of seed exchanges and seed sources, as well as a rundown on the whole seed-saving movement, see Carolyn Jabs's book *The Heirloom Gardener*.

Following are some basic guidelines for seed savers.

1. Learn to recognize plant diseases since some of them, particularly the viral ones, are transmitted by seeds.

2. Always label the seed rows and packaged seeds, because our memories sometimes play tricks on us.

3. Never plant all your seeds at once; the elements might wipe you out.

4. Learn to select the best seeds for the next generation. For seed saving, select seeds from the healthiest plants and from those producing the best vegetables.

5. To maintain a strong gene pool, select seeds from a number of plants, not from just one or two. (This advice does not apply to self-pollinating varieties; see the information on beans in this chapter.)

6. Get to know the vegetable families; members of the same family often cross-pollinate.

7. Only mature, ripe seeds will be viable.

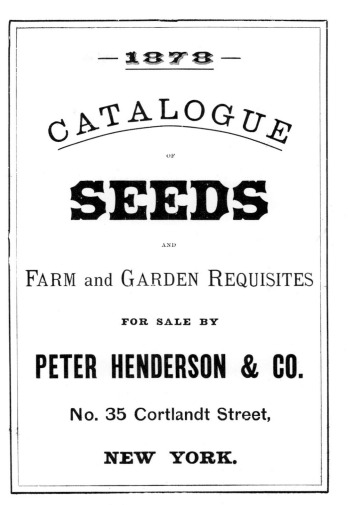

— 1878 —

CATALOGUE

OF

SEEDS

AND

FARM and GARDEN REQUISITES

FOR SALE BY

PETER HENDERSON & CO.

No. 35 Cortlandt Street,

NEW YORK.

Storing Seeds

Seeds must be stored carefully to ensure that they germinate in the next season. The greatest enemy of seed viability is moisture, so be sure to dry the seeds thoroughly before storing them. A good test of moisture content is to bite the seed; if you can't dent it, it's probably dry enough.

Another enemy is heat. Seeds must be stored in a cool, dry, dark place, or, if sufficiently dry and in a sealed container, seeds can be frozen too. They will stay viable for years in a freezer if properly packaged. Also, freezing helps protect the seeds from insects, not an uncommon problem of seed savers. (Don't freeze beans or peas, though; they need more air than freezing provides.)

Saving Beans

Beans are the easiest vegetable seeds to save. Most beans are self-pollinating, so you don't have to worry about cross-pollination when you plant them. In fact, you'll be able to grow 2 or 3 varieties with very few pollination problems. John Withee, one of this nation's most devoted seed savers, plants 250 varieties of beans every summer. He suggests planting varieties that are very different side by side; then, if any crossing does occur, the seeds that result will look quite different and you'll know that your selected variety has been altered. When harvesttime approaches, start choosing the plants that are the healthiest. With *snap* beans, let some of the healthy plants mature. They will be mature about six weeks after the eating stage. With *dry* bean varieties, allow them to mature as you would ordinarily. Beans usually ripen from the bottom to the top. Pick them as soon as the pods start to crack, so the beans won't fall to the ground and get damp. Don't pick the beans right after it has rained.

Do not save beans from diseased plants. Diseases borne by bean seeds are anthracnose and bacterial blight. The symptoms of anthracnose are small brown spots that enlarge to sunken black spots. Bacterial blight is characterized by dark green spots on the pods that slowly become dry and brick red. The most bothersome pest of bean seeds is the weevil.

After you thoroughly dry the bean seeds, package them in a breathable container, label them, and freeze them for for twenty-four hours to kill the weevils. Then put them in a cold, dark place. That's all there is to it.

John Withee has saved hundreds of heirloom varieties of beans. Here he poses with a box containing only a portion of his many varieties.

Sources of Information

Books

Bubel, Nancy. *The Seed Starter's Handbook.* Emmaus, Pa.: Rodale Press, 1978. Basic information on how to start most plants from seed as well as valuable botanical information on how to select and save your own seeds. A must for seed savers.

Fell, Derek. *Vegetables: How to Select, Grow, and Enjoy.* Tucson, Ariz.: H.P. Books, 1982. A marvelous compendium of basic vegetable growing.

Jabs, Carolyn. *The Heirloom Gardener.* San Francisco: Sierra Club Books, 1984. The definitive book on heirloom gardening. Covers the history of seed saving, gives sources of seeds as well as information on how to save seeds.

Jeavons, John, and Leler, Robin. *The Seed Finder.* Willits, Calif.: Jeavons-Leler Press, 1983. Detailed guide on where to find many of the old-time varieties.

Koopowitz, Harold, and Kaye, Hilary. *Plant Extinction—A Global Crisis.* Washington, D.C.: Stone Wall Press, 1983. The most thorough and complete book about our endangered ecosystem.

Mooney, Pat Roy. *Seeds of the Earth.* Ottawa, Canada: Inter Pares, 1979. A global look at the problem of the shrinking gene pool of edible plants.

Vilmorin-Andrieux, MM. *The Vegetable Garden.* Palo Alto, Calif.: Jeavons-Leler Press. Reprint 1976. A marvelous reprint of a classic that was first printed in 1885. It is a description of the old varieties, with information on how to grow hundreds of them. I counted fifty-five pages on peas alone.

Catalogs

Rural Advancement Fund
P.O. Box 1029
Pittsboro, NC 27312
Ask for "The Second Graham Center Seed and Nursery Directory"—a valuable catalog of seed companies that carry open-pollinated varieties of seeds. Catalog $2.

Demonstration Gardens

Many historic gardens grow heirloom vegetables and are interesting to visit. A list of these gardens is available from the Association of Living Historical Farms and Museums, c/o The Smithsonian, Washington, DC 20560.

Genesee Country Museum
P.O.Box 1819
Rochester, NY 14603
This demonstration garden is one of the most active and offers helpful information to those new to heirloom gardening.

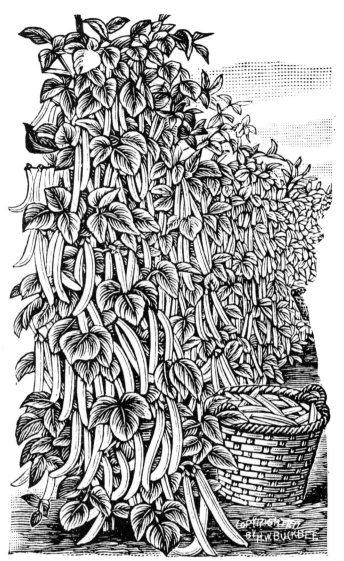

Monticello
P.O. Box 316
Charlottesville, VA 22902
Researchers are working hard to restore the
vegetable garden at Monticello. It reflects as
closely as possible the era and genius of one of
our nation's most inspired gardeners: Thomas
Jefferson. Visitors are welcome.

Nurseries

The seed companies listed below carry heirloom, open-pollinated varieties of vegetables.
Most of these companies offer seed exchanges,
as does the magazine *Gardens for All*, 180
Flynn Avenue, Burlington, VT 05401.

G. Seed Company
P.O. Box 702
Tonasket, WA 98855
G. Seeds offers a nice selection of heirloom
beans, corn, tomatoes, and other vegetables.
The company is willing to swap with you for
varieties they don't have.

J.L. Hudson, Seedsman
P.O. Box 1058
Redwood City, CA 94064
This seed company sells only open-pollinated
varieties and has a large selection.

Johnny's Selected Seeds
Albion, ME 04910
Johnny's sells seeds of many open-pollinated
vegetables, particularly those that do well in
northern climates.

Redwood City Seed Company
P.O. Box 361
Redwood City, CA 94064
Redwood carries a very large selection of open-
pollinated, heirloom vegetables and the seed of
many fruit trees. A brochure that covers heirlooms is available.

Seeds Blum
Idaho City Stage
Boise, ID 83707
Jan Blum raises her own seeds for many of the
old varieties that are being dropped by larger
seed companies. She also runs a seed exchange.

Seed Exchanges

A saved seed should be a shared seed. Help spread the wealth; join a seed exchange. Help spread the word; the more people who save and trade their seeds, the more seeds we all will have.

Native Seeds/SEARCH
3950 West New York Drive
Tucson, AZ 85745
This organization is devoted to seeking out and keeping in cultivation seeds from Southwest native crops as well as their wild relatives. A yearly membership is $10, which includes a newsletter. Seeds of these natives are available for a small fee.

Seed Savers Exchange
c/o Kent Whealy
203 Rural Avenue
Decorah, IA 52101
This is the place to start if you are interested in seed saving. Join Kent and hundreds of others in this membership organization. Membership is $6 for U.S. residents; $8 for Canadian residents. Membership entitles you to a directory of seed savers and what they want to trade, as well as information on seed saving. The directory is probably the most exciting seed catalog you will ever see; however, don't order seeds unless you are dedicated to growing and preserving these heirlooms.

Consumer Note

Seed saving is done primarily by enthusiastic gardeners and small seed companies, so there is a variation in the gardening skill of the growers and in the seeds. You might be exchanging seeds with an old-time gardener who could run circles around the average seedsman, or you could be exchanging seeds with a new gardener. The new gardener may not know how to recognize virus symptoms, say, or how to prevent cross-pollination. Be forewarned that although this has not been a large problem, there is a slight chance that you may get poor quality seeds, seed-borne diseases, or seeds that were not properly stored.

California quail

Chapter 6
The Wildlife Garden

If you have never experienced living near buffaloes and eagles, you certainly don't miss their presence. In fact, you probably are not even aware of their ever having been around. Nevertheless, those creatures, as well as many others, were once a part of our habitat. It could be, for example, that there was a buffalo migration path through your front yard. Or perhaps your yard was once the nesting site of eagles.

With a little research and imagination you can partially restore the natural state of your land by putting in plants native to your specific locale. The net effect will be not only a preserve for the plants you choose, but a protected retreat for many of the wildlife species that live in your ecological niche.

Your yard will be part of the ark, instead of a large expanse of Kentucky bluegrass with a mustache of shrubs across the front of the house, when you plant a number of different species that need preserving and that will serve as habitat for native animal species. If your design is well conceived, the result will be beautiful and maybe more unusual than any

other yard in your neighborhood. In addition, it will give you pleasure and help preserve species.

There are a number of tacks you can take when planting with the express purpose of protecting your area's wildlife species. For example, if you are interested in providing a habitat for birds, butterflies, and small mammals, you can set up your yard as a haven for them. Another, less radical option is a conventional yard augmented with a bird house for purple martins, and, instead of forsythia, maybe a hedge of viburnum or elderberries for the cedar waxwings, and a colorful border with hollyhocks for the painted lady butterflies.

If you want to create a true wildlife preserve, you'll need to think not only about what kinds of wildlife you do want to attract but also which animals you don't want to attract. A few years ago a native brown bear meandered out of the wilderness south of the San Francisco area. He kept himself busy for days foraging up and down the creeks and in suburban backyards. Cocktail parties were arranged on the chance that he might appear. Obviously, there's "wild" life, then there's wildlife. Bears, mountain lions, and wolves are not the wildlife I expect you will want in your yard.

Still, even the less-alarming species, in terms of their size and wildness, require some careful consideration. For example, our backyard, even though in a suburban area, is near a creek. Occasionally our visitors include an opossum, a raccoon, an owl, and a bevy of quail. Unfortunately we also have too many squirrels and, occasionally, a skunk. A squirrel can go through a ripe apricot tree like a bejeweled matron picking over a box of mixed chocolates, tasting or knocking down ten apricots for every one it eats. Squirrels rip apart my macrame plant hangers to make their nests, and occasionally a raccoon gets into the garbage can. Sometimes we see a roof rat, and we know neighbors who had to spend the night in a motel waiting for a skunk to go back out through the "doggy" door at home. With wildlife you can't put up a turnstile and let in only those animals you want.

Fortunately, though, if you really want wildlife to be a part of your landscape, you can usually make the necessary arrangements to encourage the species you want and to discourage or guard against those you don't want. Raccoons can be kept out of garbage cans by using certain kinds of lids. Skunks can be prevented from getting under the house by screening all house vents. When squirrels overpopulate, you can control their numbers by trapping and relocating them. Encouraging (and discouraging) wildlife requires some preplanning on your part, but it is worth the effort. Despite my cursing at the squirrels, I remember the joy of watching baby hummingbirds learn to fly, of awaiting the arrival of the migrating woodpecker that visits us and hammers on the trees every year in May, and of seeing, one foggy morning, a stag staring in the kitchen window. I wouldn't trade any of those moments. However, realistic expecta-

Above While it is great to feed wildlife, you can't put up a turnstyle and let in only those animals you want. If skunks are prevalent in your area, pet food left outside is sure to attract them.

Opposite Purple martins are extremely beneficial in controlling insects in the garden. You don't have to provide them with a mansion as the owners of Middleton Gardens in South Carolina have done; a simple structure built well above the ground will suffice. At the end of this chapter is a list of books about how to attract birds and how to build a bird house for purple martins.

tions and good planning are definitely the keys to a successful wildlife garden.

I'd like to say a few words about expectations. Whereas we love birds, small fuzzy mammals, and Bambi, we generally say "yuck" to spiders, toads, and snakes. This brings me back to the main reason for changing our yards: As far as I am concerned, it is to reinstitute as closely as possible whole, natural habitats. A successful habitat is one that has as many niches filled as possible; some of the creatures that we are not fond of do belong. We all like butterflies, and many of them are becoming endangered because we don't like caterpillars or chewed foliage and flowers. Since the caterpillar has to eat foliage in order to become a butterfly, we have to tolerate chewed foliage or give up butterflies. Try hard to separate facts from prejudices. The black widow spider, the rattlesnake, and poison ivy are hazardous; but garter snakes, daddy longlegs,

and most toads are not. There are many books on how to encourage birds and small mammals, but there are no books devoted to how to encourage spiders, toads, and snakes. You will have to use your own senses and observation to teach you how.

All wildlife needs food, water, shelter, and areas for reproducing and rearing young. If you have a yard that is near a fairly wild area and has many mature trees and shrubs, you will need only to provide water in dry times and extra food in the winter. A more typical yard in this country, however, is the suburban yard— a large lawn, a few clipped exotic shrubs, and a small tree or two. If this is your situation, then you have many decisions to make. It will probably be necessary to remove some species and plant others, provide feeders and water sources, and reevaluate landscaping procedures because they are at cross-purposes with your goal.

How to Change Minds and the Landscape

Begin at the beginning. That is, recognize that by changing the emphasis in your mind and, consequently, in your yard, you are making a radical departure from the usual people-oriented garden—its goals, techniques, and procedures. So radical a change requires awareness, information, planning, sensitivity, and, sometimes, even tact.

You must realize that you will have to continually monitor and "translate" information you get from garden books and other sources because garden information in this country is primarily people oriented. The subjugation of nature, not the encouragement of natural systems, is often the goal. Because you are not living in the wilderness, a compromise usually must be made. For example, many woodpeckers need dead branches or trees to nest in, but garden books tell you to remove dead trees or to trim off dead branches for the good of the tree. You will have to determine your priorities. If the tree is your favorite or if it shades a south wall in summer or if the dead branch could fall and hurt someone, then it should probably be removed. Be aware also of your redefinition of the word "pests." An insect defined as a pest in a people-oriented landscape may be defined as food for spiders and birds in a wildlife-oriented one. Many such translations will have to be made.

Be realistic in choosing your goals. If all your neighbors spray their yards with pesticides and think that the only proper landscape scheme is a lawn and some clipped shrubs, then obviously you must scale down your expectations. If starlings are moving in or if neighborhood cats are having a field day, then changes will have to be made. As a rule, it usually pays to start slowly and continually monitor the situation, making changes when necessary.

For neighbors who are used to mown lawns and clipped hedges and who may be unnerved by your installing a thicket of shrubs and vines and putting in a meadow of unmown grasses and wildflowers, a little tact and discretion on your part will pay off. My inclination in the case where neighbors may be unsympathetic is to start slowly and to share your enthusiasm. Talk about your ideas for providing a home for a family of cardinals or robins. If you make your yard attractive and share your enthusiasm with your neighbors, you will probably recruit them to your cause, then everyone will benefit because the more neighbors that are involved, the more wildlife you all will have—and the more habitat the wildlife will have.

Join the National Audubon Society and the National Wildlife Federation. There are many good books about wildlife and a number of nurseries devoted to providing plants for wildlife (see the lists at the end of this chapter).

The National Wildlife Federation's Backyard Wildlife Habitat Program is composed of thousands of families who have decided to give wildlife a major place in their yards. If you meet a few requirements, for $2 you may register your yard and get information and encouragement for your garden. The program is for homeowners with three acres or less or for those with larger lots who want to register only a portion of three acres or less. The goals of the

program are to provide more refuges for indigenous animals and to share and document experiences so that others can profit from the experiences. To get information and an application for this program, write to Backyard Wildlife Habitat Program, National Wildlife Federation, 1412 16th Street NW, Washington, DC 20036. The application asks you to describe what steps you are taking to encourage wildlife. Once you are registered, you will receive useful information on how to get started and an occasional issue of *The Backyard Wildlifer,* a newsletter to keep you up to date on successful wildlife gardening techniques and on the latest books.

Before turning to the practical aspects of creating a wildlife preserve, I want to remind you that plant species are as crucial to the ark as animal species, perhaps more so. The reason for creating a wildlife preserve is not solely to protect endangered animals but to perpetuate the complex interdependence between plants and animals that is the hallmark of a natural system.

Above This yard in Colorado recently became the two-thousandth yard in the National Wildlife Association's Backyard Wildlife Program. It is filled with sheltering and fruit-bearing shrubs and is visited by many animals and birds.

Opposite Elderberries are a great favorite of birds—with what is left over you can make fabulous jam.

Planning and Preparation

Begin by assessing your yard. A large rural lot has many more options than a city lot, but both can make a valuable contribution and be augmented with a bird feeder and a bird bath and shrubs and trees that feed wild birds. Most people think about birds but forget about butterflies, bumblebees, and other insects. Select your flowers with insects in mind, and not just at their nectar stage. While it's fun to watch a butterfly flit around, the caterpillar must be fed. Dill, parsley, and fennel are food for the colorful larvae of many swallowtail butterflies. If you don't plant and share your dill, you probably won't have the swallowtails flitting around your zinnias.

Next, get some graph paper and plan in detail the changes that are to be made. Measure your yard and lay it out to scale on paper. Plan wildlife areas, clusters of shrubs, maybe a hedgerow, even a small pool. Select plants that will provide food all through the year. When doing your layout, it is helpful to have some of the basic texts that cover landscaping for wildlife. Also, get some nature guides for your part of the country. Collecting this resource material can be a family project. See the lists of books at the end of this chapter and at the ends of Chapters 1, 2, 3, 4, and 10.

Planting for Wildlife

Birds and animals need shelter. Your yard will be more hospitable if you provide many of the following: (1) many levels of vegetation, including low shrubs, ground covers, tall shrubs, and small and large trees; (2) vines; (3) plants with thorns to give protection from cats; (4) trees, stumps, and dead trees to provide nesting sites for woodpeckers, owls, and raccoons (If they did not die of a disease that will spread to other trees, keep as many tree stumps and dead trees as possible, but eliminate those that are near buildings and places where chil-

dren play and people walk.); and (5) bird houses, especially in young yards with few trees.

In addition, try to avoid the manicured yard because well-manicured yards eliminate many hiding places. Shrubbery should be allowed to branch to the ground; and leaf litter and old grass stalks are valuable for nesting materials and for burrowing mammals and insects.

Wildlife is attracted to a yard that provides food and water. Keep in mind that most animals and birds need food all year round. Use plants that seed or fruit at different times of the year. Food can be provided by food-producing plants and by bird and animal feeders. Again, avoid the manicured yard. Because I allow my cosmos and large marigolds to go to seed, my garden is visited all summer by flocks of yellow finches who scramble for the seeds. Leaf litter provides food for worms, who in turn provide food for robins. Leave a few aphids on some of your plants to provide food for lacewings and ladybugs.

Small fountains with moving water often attract more wildlife than still water, and they have the advantage of creating fewer mosquito problems. If you can put in a small pond with fish, which help control mosquitoes, you will have the best situation. If your source of water

Opposite Wildlife needs food, water, and shelter. Notice how bird houses and feeders are spotted around the yard. Notice, too, that almost every ornamental plant has a dual role: some provide food; others provide shelter for birds, insects, and small mammals. Also, nearly all are beautiful to look at or serve as windbreaks for the house. The vegetable garden is fenced for protection, and especially vulnerable plants, such as the strawberries, are placed close to the front door so the occupants will have some chance at the harvest.

 1. Elderberry
 2. Bayberry
 3. Winterberry
 4. Butterfly bush
 5. Viburnum
 6. Junipers, low
 7. Red maple
 8. Viburnum
 9. Blueberries
10. Strawberries in containers
11. Birches
12. Amelanchier
13. Winter creeper
14. Lilac
15. Native pines
16. Dogwood
17. Mountain ash

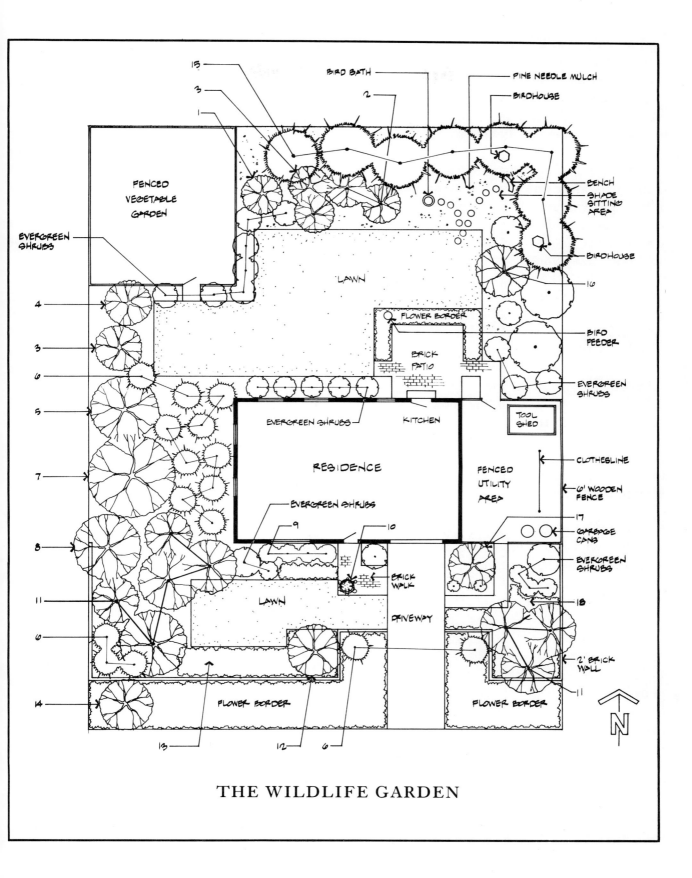

THE WILDLIFE GARDEN

is limited and still, such as a bird bath, change the water daily. Water should be out in the open, surrounded by lawn, for example, so that neighborhood cats cannot sneak up on the visiting wildlife. In the winter you may want to set up an immersion heater to keep the water from freezing.

When choosing the plants for your wildlife garden, concentrate on plants native to your area; they will attract the most wildlife. Be sure to provide a wide variety of trees, shrubs, and herbaceous plants; the more variety the more wildlife you will attract. Lawn areas surrounded by many layers of vegetation make successful wildlife gardens. There are a number of good books on the subject; one of the best is *Gardening with Wildlife,* published by the National Wildlife Federation.

Look over the model wildlife garden in this chapter to get some ideas for your garden. Notice that not just wildlife habitat is considered, but protection for the inhabitants of the house as well. The deciduous trees such as birch, red maple, and dogwood that provide food and shelter for birds have been situated where they shade the house in summer. Sheltering evergreens that provide safe nesting sites for birds are placed to form a windbreak from winter winds for the house. The vegetable garden has been fenced off from rabbits and small mammals, and if the residents want a bountiful harvest, the blueberry bushes, strawberries, and young seedlings in the vegetable garden will need the additional protection of bird netting.

The style of the yard is informal, and the shrubbery is meant to grow primarily unpruned because, as I mentioned earlier, unpruned shrubbery furnishes hiding and nesting places. The flower borders give much food to insects and birds as well as hours of pleasure to passersby. Large bowers of blooming and fruiting shrubs delight many songbirds and butterflies. Finally, bird feeders, bird houses, and a bird bath are included in the yard. These are particularly important to provide food, shelter, and water in new yards that are not yet well established and in older yards to give wildlife sustenance in the winter.

Be forewarned that most of the information for wildlife gardens is heavily weighted toward animals and is sometimes insensitive to the needs of native plants. For example, some of the plants recommended, although good sources of food for birds, can spread and crowd out acres of native plants. Native habitats are the most stable; it is equally important to preserve plants and animals.

Try to avoid planting particularly invasive weeds such as Japanese honeysuckle, Oriental bittersweet, multiflora roses, and purple loosestrife. Choose some of the plants on the following list, which includes plants that are usually well behaved. (But, again, check the list of "green invaders" on page 17 to make sure that the plants are not a problem in your particular area.) Ask local naturalists which plants on this list will be most attractive to your local birds, butterflies, and small mammals.

Opposite, clockwise from top The lowly opossum looks its best perched in a redbud tree.

A wood thrush is a welcome visitor to the garden. Plan for trees and shrubs that give nesting sites and protection.

A monarch butterfly sips from a tithonia blossom. Planting different species of flowers in your garden provides for many species of butterflies.

Page 98, clockwise from top left Many heirloom fruits, such as the 'Sonoma' melon and 'Pink Pearl' apple shown here, are extremely flavorful and should be preserved.

Jan Blum is the owner of one of the new seed companies that are interested in heirloom varieties. Here she is harvesting several of her eighty varieties of heirloom potatoes.

A close-up of some of Blum's heirloom varieties of potatoes, broccoli, cauliflower, and kale.

Page 99, clockwise from top left Brassia Edvah Loo.

Phalaenopsis Golden Sands 'Canary'.

The large white orchid is a cattleya hybrid Japhet type; the tall pink one is a *Doritaenopsis*; in the middle are three types of *Paphiopedilum*, or lady's-slipper orchids; and in the foreground are different types of *Phalaenopsis*.

Three different types of cattleya are growing in a moderate-to-warm windowsill garden. Top left, *C. Angelwalker* x *C. amethystoglossa*; lower left, *Lc. Cuiseag* 'Cuddles'; lower right, *Slc. Brillig*.

Opposite, clockwise from top left 'Old Blush' China climbing rose.

White Rugosa rose

'Cornelia' Hybrid Musk rose

Rosa damascena Trigintipetala

Plants for Birds

The following list of trees and plants will guide you in selecting plants that will attract birds to your garden.

Small Trees

Dogwood, *Cornus,* most species
Hawthorn, *Crataegus* species
Mountain ash, *Sorbus* species
Serviceberry, *Amelanchier* species

Large Trees

Birch, *Betula* species
Green ash, *Fraxinus pennsylvanica*
Hackberry, *Celtis occidentalis, C. reticulata*
Maple, *Acer rubrum*
Mimosa (silk tree), *Albizia Julibrissin*
Oak, *Quercus* species (native species in particular)
Persimmon, *Diospyros* species
Pine, *Pinus Strobus, P. edulis*
Tulip tree, *Liriodendron Tulipifera*

Vines

Bittersweet, *Celastrus scandens*
Five-leaf akebia, *Akebia quinata*
Virginia creeper, *Parthenocissus quinquefolia*
Winter creeper, *Euonymus Fortunei*

Shrubs

American cranberry bush, *Viburnum trilobum*
Cherry laurel, *Prunus Laurocerasus*
Elderberry, *Sambucus* species
Fire thorn, *Pyracantha* species
Juniper, *Juniperus* species
Myrtle, *Myrtus communis*
Rose, *Rosa* species (see Chapter 7)
Silverberry, *Elaeagnus commutata,*
    E. pungens
Winterberry, *Ilex laevigata*
Witch hazel, *Hamamelis vernalis,*
    H. virginiana

Perennials

Aster, *Aster* species
Black-eyed susan, *Rudbeckia* species
Chrysanthemum, *Chrysanthemum* species
Columbine, *Aquilegia* species
Statice, *Limonium latifolium*

Annuals

Amaranthus, *Amaranthus* species
Bachelor's-button, *Centaurea Cyanus*
Calendula, *Calendula officinalis*
Coreopsis, *Coreopsis* species
Cosmos, *Cosmos* species
Marigold, *Tagetes* species
Pink, *Dianthus* species
Sunflower, *Helianthus* species

Plants for Butterflies

Meadow and prairie gardens are wonderful habitats for butterflies, as are perennial flower borders. Consult *Theme Gardens* by Barbara Damrosch for more information. Different flowers and foliage plants attract different species of butterflies. The range of native butterflies and their food sources vary from region to region. Check with local wildlife experts to see which butterflies you are most likely to attract. Following is a list of plants that are attractive to butterflies.

Shrubs

Agave, *Agave deserti*
Blueberry, *Vaccinium* species
Butterfly bush, *Buddleia Davidii*
Ceanothus, *Ceanothus* species
Cherry, *Prunus* species
Dogwood, *Cornus* species
Lilac, *Syringa vulgaris*
Passionflower, *Passiflora* species
Spicebush, *Lindera Benzoin*
Willow, *Salix* species
Wisteria, *Wisteria* species

Perennials

Aster, *Aster* species
Chives, *Allium schoenoprasum*
Coreopsis, *Coreopsis grandiflora*
Daylily, *Hemerocallis* species
Goldenrod, *Solidago* species
Hollyhock, *Alcea rosea*
Lupine, *Lupinus* species
Phlox, *Phlox* species
Sage, *Salvia* species
Scabiosa, *Scabiosa caucasica*
Sedum, *Sedum spectabile*

Annuals

Dill, *Anethum graveolens*
Fennel, *Foeniculum vulgare*
Marigold, *Tagetes* species
Parsley, *Petroselinum* species
Stock, *Matthiola incana*
Sunflower, *Helianthus* species
Zinnia, *Zinnia* species

Protection—Just Good Sense

Foods that are appealing to humans are usually favorites of wildlife too. Therefore, if there are edible plants in your yard or your neighbors' yards, plan to protect them. If the gardens are not protected by fences, fence the areas, or don't encourage wildlife. Scarecrows are often useful (and fun to create). One way to save some of your fruit crop for yourself is to anticipate sharing it with the birds and plant extra. For example, plant two plum trees or two cherry trees and a mulberry tree instead of one plum tree or just cherries. I recommend using all three types of protection: netting, scarecrows, *and* sharing your harvest.

To make your house safe from unwanted visitors, batten down the hatches. Nail or board up crawl spaces; make sure screening is secure over vent holes in the attic and the basement. Retire doggy doors lest they become skunk doors. Garbage cans should be secured; clamped lids usually discourage raccoons, but not always. If raccoons continue to be a problem, keep the garbage cans locked in a garage, or attach a door spring to the handles of the can. Install a screen over the top of the chimney to keep swifts and bats from nesting there.

Check with the local board of health to find out if there are rats in your area. Many suburbs have them; they are not just an inner-city problem. If rats are a problem in your area, keep ivylike ground covers to a minimum and clean up debris. Don't leave trash piled around. Stack woodpiles neatly—off the ground. And, most important, don't leave food out for domestic animals.

There are many ways to protect your plants from wildlife. Here are a few. Wrap chicken wire around the trunks of young trees so the bark can't be eaten by rabbits and deer. Keep in mind that piled-up snow allows animals to reach farther up the trunk, sometimes as much as four to five feet higher. Take into account your local snowfall. Leave at least six inches of space between the wire and the trunk so that the critters can't reach in. If gophers are a problem in your area, set out young plants in chicken-wire baskets to protect the roots.

Control and protect your pets. To enjoy the benefits of wildlife in your yard, you must control your household pets. Cats are one of the biggest problems for birds and small mammals; keep them inside or put bells on their collars. Free-running dogs are a severe problem in rural and semirural areas; these pets run in packs and kill deer and other mammals, not to mention a neighbor's sheep and chickens. Pets should have their rabies shots regularly, in case they have an encounter with a rabid wild creature.

Providing for wildlife is a rewarding aspect of gardening. It is a project that will never be complete; the environment is always changing.

Rabbits are cute and sure to be a nuisance in a vegetable garden.

Sources of Information

Books

Damrosch, Barbara. *Theme Gardens*. New York: Workman Publishing, 1982. Good information on how to attract butterflies and hummingbirds to your garden.

National Wildlife Federation. *Gardening with Wildlife*. Washington, D.C.: National Wildlife Federation, 1974. A comprehensive book on the subject of gardening with wildlife. A must!

Ortho Books, Chevron Chemical Company editorial staff. *How to Attract Birds*. San Francisco: Ortho Books, 1983. Extensive information on birds and the plants that they prefer for food and shelter.

Rothschild, Miriam, and Farrell, Clive. *The Butterfly Gardener*. London: Michael Joseph, 1983. A must for butterfly lovers. It even covers raising butterflies in captivity.

Also see the books recommended at the end of the first four chapters and the Peterson field guides, which cover insects, birds, reptiles, and animals of this continent.

Nurseries

Dutch Mountain Nursery
7984 North 48th Street
Route 1
Augusta, MI 49012
This nursery has a large variety of shrubs, trees, and vines that are very valuable for wildlife. Catalog 25 cents.

Clyde Robin Seed Company, Inc.
P.O. Box 2855
Castro Valley, CA 94546
This nursery specializes in seeds of native wildflowers and shrubs. It has wildflower mixes for all parts of the country. Catalog $2. Also see the sources of information at the end of Chapter 1 for more information.

Wildlife Nurseries
P.O. Box 2724
Oshkosh, WI 54903
This company specializes in plants that provide food for wildlife, particularly for game birds and ducks. It has a good selection of seeds of plants for marshes and streamsides, and even sells tadpoles and baby ducks and turtles.

For additional information on nurseries, see the lists of nurseries at the ends of Chapters 1, 2, 3, and 4 and purchase the booklet *Nursery Source Manual*, a Brooklyn Botanic Garden publication. Send $3.05 to the Brooklyn Botanic Garden, 1000 Washington Avenue, Brooklyn, NY 11225, to obtain the booklet.

Organizations

National Audubon Society
950 Third Avenue
New York, NY 10022
This venerable old organization offers many publications with information on attracting birds to your yard.

National Wildlife Federation
1412 16th Street NW
Washington, DC 20036
An organization with a wealth of information for the homeowner who is interested in attracting wildlife.

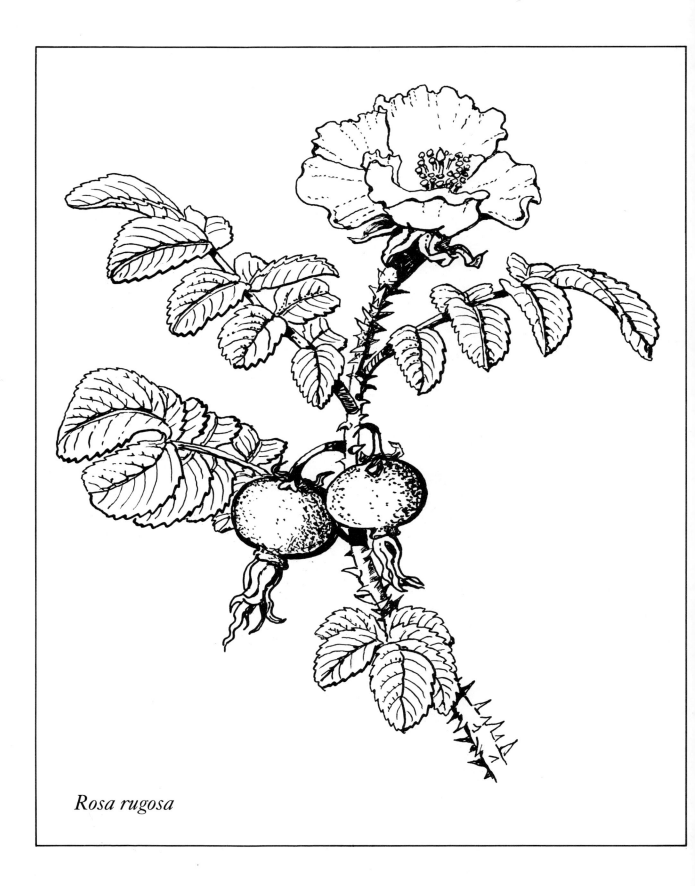

Rosa rugosa

Chapter 7
The Heritage Rose Garden

To many people, "roses" mean the old-fashioned roses of song, sonnet, and grandma's garden—roses that produce bowers of fragrant flowers, showers of shell pink petals on a warm day in June, or bouquets of rosebuds on a picket fence. These sentimental favorites bring to mind such names as Damask, Moss, Sweetbrier, and 'Maiden's Blush'. Instead of experiencing history only on paper, plant *Rosa damascena bifera* and enjoy, as did Ovid and Homer, its perfume and clear pink, double flowers. Or enjoy the ripe-apple smell of the Sweetbrier as Shakespeare may have. While these and other old roses have always been among people's favorite flowers, the recent quest for the new hybrid tea roses has meant that these old roses have been ignored for the last forty or fifty years. However, a new awakening in horticulture, fueled sometimes by nostalgia, sometimes by concern over the loss of old varieties, and often by despair at the amount of care many hybrid tea roses require, has caused a rapidly growing interest in heritage roses. The interest in and concern for heritage roses have developed none too soon. We could very well have lost a substantial amount of this antique gene pool.

Rose growing since the turn of the century has been devoted mainly to the latest hybrid tea roses. Each new introduction has been hailed as an improvement over those of previous years. Sometimes the improvements were truly improvements, and the roses were more cold tolerant or more disease resistant. Often, however, improvement simply meant different —a different color or a different bud shape. Fragrant roses, for example, are out of style, so some modern roses have no scent. Pesticides have become readily available, so some beautiful but quite disease-prone introductions were made. Water and fertilizer were plentiful, so some of the new hybrids are nourishment-greedy. The rose garden of the twentieth century is very high maintenance. And what has happened to the old-fashioned favorites? Well, some are extinct, others are still growing in grandma's garden and in old cemeteries, and a few are being propagated and sold by people like Pat Wiley, proprietor of America's best-known heritage rose nursery, Roses of Yesterday and Today.

In contrast to their hybrid cousins, many heritage roses are low-maintenance plants. In fact, according to Wiley, the most common mistake gardeners make with old roses is to treat them as they do modern hybrid tea roses. Hybrid tea roses need severe winter pruning, systematic summer removal of spent blooms, frequent fertilizing, supplemental watering, and, in most of the country, nearly weekly spraying for diseases and pests. To the contrary, once established, most old-fashioned roses are easy to care for.

According to another heritage rose authority, Beverly Dobson, *Rosa rugosa, R. rugosa alba,* and *R. rugosa Rubra* are absolutely disease-free. Further, the great majority of the old rose varieties require fewer petroleum products in the form of fertilizers and pesticides, can survive with less water, and are perfect examples of appropriate gardening.

Growing heritage roses makes sense in terms of conservation and ease of maintenance, but, more important, we should grow these roses so that generations to come, our descendants, can take a break from their computer consoles and refresh their senses with the scent of one of the heritage beauties. If we keep the Damask and Sweetbrier roses alive, our great-grandchildren will be able to have an experience in common with Shakespeare and Homer.

Pat Wiley is the owner of Roses of Yesterday and Today, one of the few nurseries devoted to heritage roses.

Heritage Roses

The rose family is vast. If you are a beginning gardener or don't want to spray your roses, choose from the following hardy types: Hybrid Musk, Autumn Damask, Damask, Gallica, Alba, Rugosa, Moss, Centifolia, Hybrid Moss, and species roses such as *Eglanteria, pendulina,* and *rubrifolia.* There are hundreds of varieties in these different classifications. If you are an experienced gardener or live in a part of the country where rose diseases are rarely a problem, you may want to choose from an even larger selection, such as the one given in Beverly Dobson's booklet on roses. Her booklet, described at the end of this chapter, gives information and availability of the majority of heritage roses.

In addition to choosing for disease resistance, you can make other choices as well when you select your heritage roses. Some types give a spectacular show of blooms once in the spring; other varieties bloom on and off throughout the growing season. A few of the old roses, such as some of the Hybrid Musks and Albas, can be grown in filtered sun, so if you have limited sun, choose one of those. If you live in a very cold area, choose from the most hardy varieties. Most of the old roses are cold tolerant, and some extremely hardy types can be grown as far north as the arctic.

Unusual and Easy-to-Grow Old Roses

Pat Wiley recommends the following old roses as being particularly disease- and pest-free.

'Delicata', Rugosa (1898). Flowers repeatedly; large double lavender pink blooms; produces large, colorful hips.

'Old Blush', China (1752). Flowers repeatedly; semidouble pink flowers.

'Perle d'Or', Polyantha (1884). Flowers repeatedly; pink to amber flowers; quite disease-free.

Rosa damascena Trigintipetala, Damask (prior to 1850). One annual flowering; cherry red flowers, red hips; disease-free plant.

'Safrano', Tea (1839). Flowers repeatedly; light apricot flowers; needs little fertilization or irrigation.

'Zephirine Drouhin', Bourbon (1868). Flowers repeatedly; bright pink flowers; no thorns; disease-free.

Modern Roses

Most modern hybrid tea roses need constant attention: spraying, fertilizing, and pruning. A few varieties are more disease resistant than the average, generally needing little spraying if planted in the right place—with full sun, good drainage, and away from a lawn where constant irrigation makes the environment too moist. Choose from the following list of fairly disease-resistant tea roses, but remember that most will require more care than their heritage cousins.

'Belinda', Hybrid Musk (1936). Flowers repeatedly; trusses of one-inch bright pink flowers; disease and pest resistant.

'Cornelia', Hybrid Musk (1925). Flowers repeatedly; coral to pink blooms; disease and pest resistant.

'Golden Fleece', Floribunda (1955). Flowers repeatedly; large yellow flowers.

'New Dawn', Climber (1930). Flowers repeatedly; pale pink flowers; disease-free foliage.

'Rosette Delizy', Tea (1922). Flowers repeatedly; yellow to red flowers; disease and pest resistant.

I asked Beverly Dobson, who gardens in New York, for her recommendations of disease-resistant, easy-to-grow, old roses, and she recommended the Rugosas, the Damasks, the Albas, the Centifolias, the Moss types, and the following varieties in particular.

'Celsiana', Damask (prior to 1750). One annual flowering; warm pink flowers.

'Leda', Painted Damask (before 1827). White or near white.

'Konigin von Danemark', Alba (1826). One annual flowering; pink.

R. gallica officinalis, Apothecary (before 1300). One annual flowering; light crimson.

'Rosa Mundi', Gallica (prior to 1581). One annual flowering; red stripes over pink ground.

Planning and Preparation

While roses can be spotted in the back of shrub borders and along walls and driveways, a rose garden has traditionally been the most graceful way to feature roses in a landscape. Roses come in many colors and shapes, and to show them off in all their glory, it helps to give them a jewellike setting. See the accompanying diagram, a good-size area organized to feature heirloom roses.

In planning your rose garden it helps if you define the area, as was done in the diagram, with a fence or boxwood hedge and paths of brick or gravel. Fencing and paths give the area form when the roses are dormant in winter, and they provide a strong design element that serves to unify the area. Rose plants, particularly the heritage varieties, have different forms and colors of flowers and need a strong design because they sometimes compete with each other for the viewer's eye. In the accompanying design, I placed Rugosa roses, with their crisp clean foliage and controlled form, in all the corners of the garden to further unify the design. You could probably use Rugosa roses in the same manner because they grow well in most parts of the country. Having laid the framework for a unified garden—paths, fencing, and the Rugosa roses—I then delighted in choosing one each of many other kinds of roses to fill in the planting beds. The resulting garden full of fragrances, representing a full spectrum of flower types and colors, shows off the great variety of the heritage rose.

Planting Roses

While most old roses are pretty tough, all perform best in good, well-drained soil and plenty of sun. Most of these rose bushes are large and need room to spread so they can be seen in all their beauty. Old roses can be situated in a rose garden or used in a landscape design. They can cover arbors, fences, and walls, or cascade over banks. Some varieties, such as some of the Rugosas, can be used as a hedge; others can stand alone as large fountain-shaped shrubs. Everywhere you use the heritage roses they produce a spectacular show of blooms and become a noteworthy focal point in the garden.

Purchase bare-root roses in late winter from local nurseries or, in the case of many of the old roses, from mail-order firms. Plant them as soon as possible after purchase. Unwrap them the night before planting and revitalize the roots with a solution of vitamin B_1.

Opposite Surround yourself with the many scents and colors of an old rose garden. The diagram shows a heritage rose garden laid out in a geometric shape, surrounded with a low hedge of lavender or boxwood to give it form throughout the seasons and to unify the area. I chose to repeat one of the sturdiest Rugosa roses, 'Delicata', in a number of places to further unify the garden. There is a wide choice of flower colors and shapes represented as well as a number of varieties that bloom throughout the whole summer.
 1. 'Delicata' (lavender)
 2. 'Safrano' (apricot)
 3. 'Konigin von Danemark' (pink)
 4. *Rosa gallica officinalis* (light crimson)
 5. 'Leda' (white)
 6. 'Penelope' (salmon pink climber)
 7. 'Perle d'Or' (amber)
 8. 'Celsiana' (pink)
 9. *Rosa damascena Trigintipetala* (red)
 10. 'Old Blush' (pink)

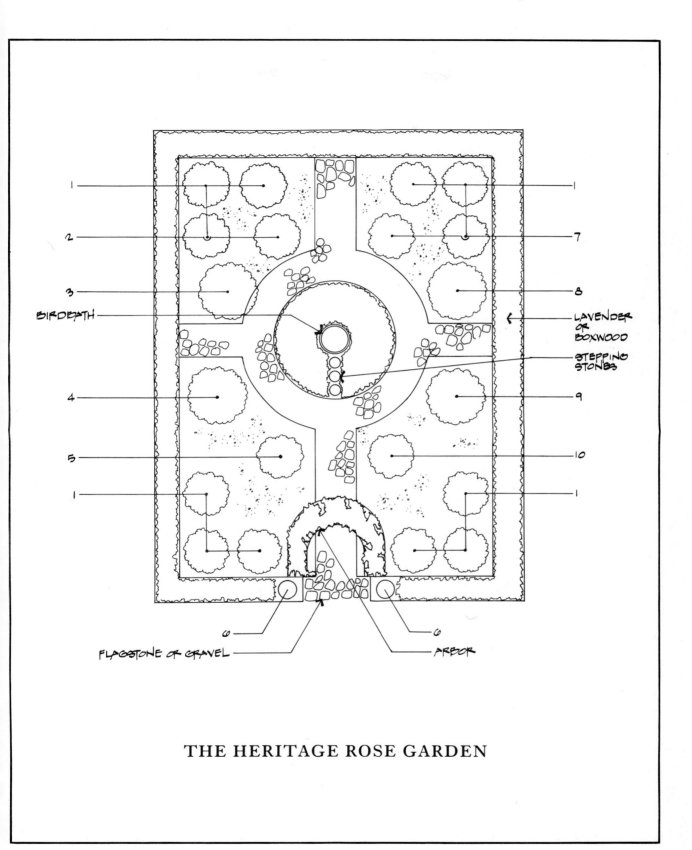

THE HERITAGE ROSE GARDEN

Dig a hole about two feet deep and at least eighteen inches across. Put two tablespoons of bone meal in the bottom of the hole, then partially fill it in with light, amended soil. Form the soil into a slight mound and gently mold the roots of the rose over the mound of soil. Fill in the rest of the hole and firm the soil around the roots, making sure the bud union (a swelling a few inches above where the roots begin) is about two inches above the soil line. Water very slowly and very thoroughly. It is critical to completely moisten the soil and to remove any air pockets. Keep your new rose moist for the first six weeks or so. After that, the watering schedule will depend on your climate. You can get general guidelines from local rose growers, but remember that in most cases old rose varieties can get along on much less water than their hybrid tea cousins. Once established, many old roses are quite drought tolerant, but to get the most blooms and lush growth in arid climates, give them an occasional deep watering.

Maintenance

Unlike hybrid tea roses, old roses should not be pruned severely. In fact, if you do prune them severely, you will probably cut off most of the buds; and, in the case of some of the large ramblers, you will get only a puny show instead of a large billowing mass of blooms. Prune heritage roses primarily to shape them, not to induce flowering. Varieties of old roses that bloom only once a year should be pruned *after* they bloom, not before. The varieties that bloom repeatedly throughout the year should be lightly pruned in late winter or early spring. Pat Wiley says, "Study your roses so that you begin to know their personalities. Some of the older varieties that bloom repeatedly should not be pruned except to remove weak or dead growth . . . their beauty is in a large plant with hundreds of small flowers, and if you prune them like you would a hybrid tea or floribunda,

you will not get a mass of blooms." After about two or three years, it is a good idea to remove a few old canes from all your roses because the new ones grow from the base of the plant.

Your old roses will benefit from yearly applications of manure or compost. If the foliage becomes pale, use supplemental applications of nitrogen. Most of the old roses are very pest and disease tolerant; that is, if they become diseased or pest ridden, they won't look their best, but they can *live through* the attacks. Some of the varieties on the list, particularly the Rugosas, almost never get diseases. Find out which rose diseases are a problem in your area and choose the varieties that are immune or resistant to them. Spider mites and aphids can occasionally be a problem on roses. Again, they won't kill the old-timers, but if looks are critical, you may want to spray occasionally with Safer's agricultural soap.

Moss rose

If you would be happy for a week, take a wife:
if you would be happy for a month, kill your pig:
but if you would be happy all your life, plant a
garden.

An Old Chinese Saying

Sources of Information

Books

Brooklyn Botanic Garden Handbooks. *Roses.* Vol. 6, no. 1. Brooklyn, N.Y.: Brooklyn Botanic Garden, 1980. A good, inexpensive, basic book on rose growing.

Damrosch, Barbara. *Theme Gardens.* New York: Workman Publishing, 1982. This book includes the plans for a marvelous old rose garden as one of its many gardens and information on a number of the old roses.

Griffiths, Trevor. *My World of Old Roses.* London: Whitcoulls, 1983. A delightful book that covers the whole range of old roses.

A large selection of books on old roses is available from Bell's Book Store, Attention: Barbara Worl, 536 Emerson Street, Palo Alto, CA 94301.

For more information on old roses and where to obtain them, send for the booklet *Combined Rose List 1982* by Beverly Dobson. It covers roses in commerce and cultivation, the rose registration since *Modern Roses 8,* as well as where to locate hard-to-find roses. Write to Beverly Dobson, 215 Harriman Road, Irvington, NY 10533. The cost of the pamphlet is $5.

Demonstration Gardens

Following is a list of public heritage rose gardens. The best time of the year to visit these gardens is in May and June.

Alfred L. Boerner Botanical Gardens
Hales Corners, WI 53130

Empire Mine State Park
Grass Valley, CA 95945

Mormon Museum
Salt Lake City, UT 84150

Mount Vernon
Mount Vernon, VA 22121

Reinisch Rose Garden
Gages Park
4320 West 10th Street
Topeka, KS 66604

Nurseries

Dynarose Limited (formerly Ellesmere)
Brooklin, Ontario L0B 1C0
Canada

Pickering Nurseries
670 Kingston Road
Pickering, Ontario L1V 1A6
Canada

Roses of Yesterday and Today (formerly
   Tillotson's)
802 Brown's Valley Road
Watsonville, CA 95076
Catalog $2. Send an additional 88 cents if you
want it mailed first class.

Organizations

If you are interested in joining Heritage Roses,
the heritage rose society, contact the member
nearest you.

Northeast:
Lily Shohan
R.D. 1
Clinton Corners, NY 12514

Northcentral:
Henry Najat
Route 3
Monroe, WI 53566

Northwest:
Jerry Fellman
947 Broughton Way
Woodburn, OR 97071

Southwest:
Miriam Wilkins
925 Galvin Drive
El Cerrito, CA 94530

Southcentral:
Vickie Jackson
122 Bragg Street
New Orleans, LA 70124

Southeast:
Charles G. Heremias
2103 Johnstone Street
Newberry, SC 29108

Consumer Note

Avoid planting the old multiflora roses. Their growth is rampant, and they have become a serious invader in large parts of the East and Northwest. Their thickets are impenetrable, and birds spread the seeds.

A wonderful way to acquire some of the old roses is to visit old cemeteries and to ask permission to take cuttings from some of the heritage roses that have been planted there through the years. Do not plant cuttings of Moss, Alba, Damask, Gallica, or species roses directly in the ground; graft them to a rootstock such as 'Dr. Huey'. Many of the old roses are so vigorous that they become rampant if they are not grafted onto a more contained rootstock.

Birds occasionally spread rose seeds from many of the old varieties. According to Pat Wiley, though, it is not generally a problem because birds usually eat the seeds before they are completely ripe. However, if your yard is adjacent to a wild area, keep an eye out for rose seedlings in the vicinity of your roses. If you see many seedlings, remove them and the parent bush as well.

Cypripedium reginae

Chapter 8
The Orchid Garden

Orchids have a reputation for being exotic and difficult to grow. But, in fact, the orchid family, the largest family of flowering plants, with more than 35,000 species, contains some species that are so easy to grow that in many parts of the world people keep a few orchid plants just for their delight. Most are no more expensive than the average house plant. Their fanciful shapes, incredible colors, and unusual growth habits—some hang from trees—have long fascinated humans. Several hundred years ago tropical types were first introduced into Europe. Because they were rare, they developed a prestigious reputation. And because people believed orchids had to be kept in greenhouses, growing them became a hobby of the rich. The wealthy collectors became obsessed with imported varieties and put many orchid species on the road to extinction.

In the 1800s, orchids were so popular that auctions in Liverpool and London attracted a great deal of publicity. Orchid prices soared, with buyers often paying $500 for a single plant. Because people did not know how to grow them, orchids died by the thousands. English gardeners thought that plants coming from the tropics needed a hot, humid environment, so they placed orchids in stoves. The stoves combined heavily painted glass, coal fires, and hot-brick flues to simulate tropical conditions. There was no ventilation, and the bricks were doused continually with water to produce a steamy atmosphere. So many thousands of orchids died that one nobleman remarked that England had become the "grave of tropical orchids." Even though orchids died by the thousands, the novelty and beauty of those that survived inspired people to import still more.

Today not only the orchids, but the habitats that support them, are endangered. Thus one good reason to grow orchids is to provide a habitat for these lovely plants at a time when their own natural ecosystems are being destroyed by the inexorable press of land development.

Many varieties of orchids thrive in the house and, when given the right conditions, require no more care than other blooming house plants. In addition, with the proliferation of solar greenhouses, the subject of greenhouse-grown orchids becomes timely. Many of the cool-climate orchids thrive under cool greenhouse conditions; others tolerate or thrive in warm greenhouse conditions. The type of orchids you can grow depends on what kind of solar greenhouse you have and in what temperature range you keep it. Orchids rarely have pest problems that necessitate spraying.

I purposefully chose orchids over many other endangered species, such as cactuses and succulents, to illustrate that hybrids have a place in our garden plans. There is a growing fear that we are overrelying on hybrid plants. As a result, people categorically reject hybrids. The issue of hybrids in horticulture is a complex one. On the one hand, it is true that we have overrelied on hybrids in the vegetable garden (see the discussion of this subject in Chapter 5). On the other hand, the emergence of hybrid-orchid growing in this country has taken some of the pressure off the plants in the wild by cloning and propagating many of the wild species and hybridizing new plants, thereby producing a huge selection of fanciful, fairly easy-to-grow plants.

The number of choices available to the orchid grower far surpasses that of most other types of plants. With roses one gets a wide selection of colors and a few shapes; with fuschias and begonias, the same; but with orchids nature outdoes herself. Orchid flowers come in shapes so outrageous they are completely beyond human imagination. Orchids are festooned with plumes and pouches, protuberances and ruffles; the colors range from jade green to sunshine yellow, lavender, pink, orange, red, magenta, even brown. Some have blotches; some have stripes; others are crystal clear. Nowhere in the plant kingdom is there such variety.

Planning and Preparation

Orchids are herbaceous (nonwoody) perennials that occur as vines or clumping grasslike plants. Some bear a single, and usually spectacular, flower; others have many flowers. They grow in habitats from tropical rain forests to alpine meadows, from bogs to semidesert, and from sea level to 14,000 feet elevation. Most orchids are easy to grow once their basic requirements are known and met; others, however, are extremely difficult to grow.

Some orchids grow in soil and are referred to as "terrestrial"; their root systems have adapted to porous soils and humus. Other orchids grow on trees and are known as "epiphytes." Their roots have adapted to their aerial habitat. Good drainage is usually the key to healthy orchids; therefore, orchid nurseries sell a fast-draining potting mix blended especially for orchids. For some of the epiphytes there is no soil at all, just shredded bark or coconut fiber.

While some orchid varieties can be grown outdoors in some parts of this country, most should be treated as house plants or grown in a greenhouse. Many are well suited to the solar greenhouse. Orchid-growing temperatures are described by three designations: warm—daytime temperatures 75 to 85 degrees F., night 65 to 70; intermediate—daytime temperatures 70 to 80 degrees F., night 55 to 65; and cool—daytime temperatures 65 to 75 degrees F., night 50 to 55.

To bloom well, orchids need quite a bit of light. They will not grow well in a dark corner of a room; instead, they should be placed fairly near a bright window that faces east, south, or west. Plants should not receive hot, midday, summer sun. If orchids get too much sun, they turn yellow; if they get too little, they turn deep green and develop a soft, floppy growth habit. Nursery catalogs usually describe an orchid's light requirements as: bright—4,000 to 5,000 foot-candles (a southern or western window); moderate—1,500 to 4,000 foot-candles (a southern, western, or eastern window); or semi-shady—500 to 1,500 foot-candles (vary the distance between the plant and any window). About 3,000 foot-candles of light seem to be suitable for most orchids.

Most orchids like fairly humid conditions (60 to 65 percent humidity) and no strong drafts. These requirements can be met easily by placing the orchid containers on trays filled with pebbles and a half inch of water. Do not situate the plants near doors.

Purchase one of the beginning orchid-growing books recommended at the end of this chapter; most are not expensive. Assess the conditions in your home or greenhouse and choose the orchids that best fit those conditions. In addition, include at least one cattleya in your selection because it is the standard in orchid growing. Often directions for growing orchids will tell you what to do in relation to cattleya cultivation.

Even before you consider their fanciful shapes and wondrous color variations, you have to make many decisions in the process of selecting the orchids you want to grow. I asked Steve Hawkins at Rod McLellan's Acres of Orchids to choose ten readily available orchids that are suitable for beginning orchid growers. The following two indoor orchid gardens are his recommendations.

Two Windowsill Gardens

One garden is for houses that are kept on the cool side in the winter; the second is for houses that are kept warmer in winter or for those that are in warm parts of the country, such as in Florida or Hawaii.

First, there are some general guidelines that pertain to both gardens. For example, Hawkins has chosen both an east-facing and a south-facing exposure to show you how each is handled. The east-facing is optimum, but a south-

or west-facing window would be all right if you cover it with a sheer curtain to cut down on some of the bright sunlight. Make sure that the plant's leaves do not touch the window; the glass will be too cold for the plant. In addition, you should use a circulating fan to keep the air near the windows from becoming too cold. The fan will benefit the residents too because it will circulate the air, preventing the hot air from rising to the ceiling and the cold air from lying on the floor. Hawkins suggests a windowsill approximately eighteen inches wide for displaying the orchids. (A table or counter at the window would work well also.) To insure that the humidity around the plants is sufficient, he suggests placing the pots on trays that have pebbles in them, then filling the trays with water. The pebbles and water are not necessary if your house is equipped with a humidifier. Because orchids do not have lush foliage, they tend to look bare when grown by themselves. You will notice that the arrangements suggested by Hawkins leave room for other house plants that will grow under the same conditions.

The "Warm" Orchid Garden

For warm to intermediate greenhouses and homes, where daytime temperatures are between 70 and 80 degrees F., and nighttime temperatures are 60 degrees F. or warmer, choose a site where the temperatures are consistently warm and where there are no cold drafts or days when the temperature may drop to near freezing. An occasional 55-degree night is tolerable but not ideal. The orchids in the garden are described in the list below. The tallest plants and the varieties requiring the most light are located nearest the window. These orchid varieties bloom at different times of the year and will combine well with coleus, caladium, and philodendron.

Cattleya Greenwich, 'Cover Girl'. Pure green with a splash of purple at the edge of the labellum. Strong stems; blooms in the summer and fall. Intermediate temperature; moderate light.

Cattleya Gloriette, 'Superba'. Large blooms of light lavender. Dark purple labellum with a golden throat. Blooms in the late summer. Intermediate temperature; moderate light.

Phalaenopsis Toni Featherstone, 'Falcon Castle'. Dark pink striping on a pink background. Bold magenta-spotted labellums. Intermediate to warm temperature; semishady light.

Paphiopedilum Makuli. Blooms prolifically. White dorsal with green striping. Broad petals with delicate, chestnut spotting. Bronze pouch. Variegated foliage. Blooms in the summer and fall. Intermediate to warm temperature; semi-shady light.

Oncidium Carnival Costume, 'Summer Sprite'. Compact plants with a profusion of one-foot spikes at maturity. Rich gold with chestnut markings. Blooms in the summer. Intermediate temperature; moderate light.

The "Cool" Orchid Garden

This orchid garden is for a cool house, one where the winter temperatures range from 50 to 75 degrees F., or for an outdoor garden in a mild climate. The tallest plants and the ones that need the most light are nearest the window. The following selection of orchids will bloom at different times of the year and will combine well with different kinds of ivy and kalanchoe and grape ivy (*Cissus*).

Laelia Canariensis, 'Austin'. Produces silky soft yellow stars atop a foot-long stem. Blooms in the winter. Intermediate to cool temperature; moderate to bright light or outside in partial shade in mild climates.

Cymbidium Siempre, 'Summer Green'. Unusual summer bloomer. Icy green with delicate red lip markings and straight, upright spikes. Fragrant. Cool greenhouse; bright light or outdoors in partial shade in mild climates.

Above There are orchids with wondrous shapes; among them is this yellow fringed native, *Platanthera ciliaris*.

Opposite Orchids can be grown indoors on a shelf or table located near either a south- or east-facing window. Put up a sheer curtain if you have a south-facing window so the sunlight will not burn the orchid foliage. To give substance and variety to the window garden, include other kinds of house plants. Here the warm window garden includes coleus and caladium; the cool window garden has ivy and kalanchoe.

Warm Orchid Garden
1. *Phalaenopsis* Toni Featherstone, 'Falcon Castle'
2. *Cattleya* Gloriette, 'Superba'
3. *Oncidium* Carnival Costume, 'Summer Sprite'
4. *Paphiopedilum* Makuli
5. *Cattleya* Greenwich, 'Cover Girl'

Cool Orchid Garden
6. *Odontocidium* Big Mac, 'Saragossa'
7. *MacLellanara* Pagan Love Song, 'Golden Realm'
8. *Cymbidium* Siempre, 'Summer Green'
9. *Laelia Canariensis*, 'Austin'

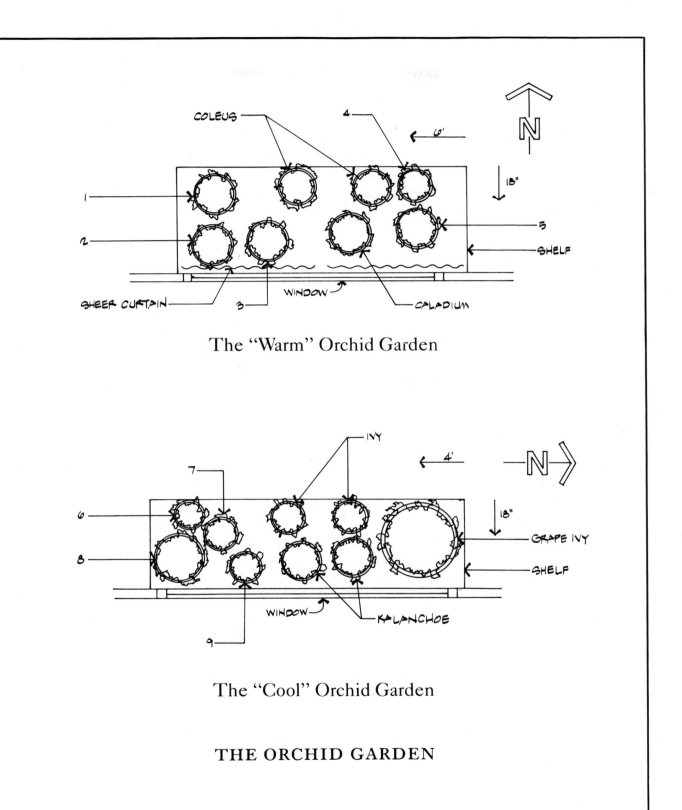

The "Warm" Orchid Garden

The "Cool" Orchid Garden

THE ORCHID GARDEN

Cymbidium Hunter's Point, 'Sunset'. Large blooms of gold to orange with red veining and barred lip. Blooms early to midseason. Two spikes per new bulb are not unusual. Cool greenhouse with bright light or outdoors with partial shade in mild climates. (This plant is not recommended for indoor growing.)

Odontocidium Big Mac, 'Saragossa'. Sprays of long-lasting chartreuse yellow with chestnut spotting. Flowers two or three times per year. Extremely strong grower. Cool to intermediate temperature; semishady light indoors or outside in heavy shade in mild climates.

MacLellanara Pagan Love Song, 'Golden Realm'. Three-to-four-foot spikes of iridescent chartreuse yellow stars with dark chocolate markings. Flowers four inches across. Blooms in the winter and spring. Intermediate to cool temperature; moderate light or outside in heavy shade in mild climates.

Maintenance

If conditions are right—proper lighting and humidity, good potting soil—orchids are quite simple to take care of. McLellan's Acres of Orchids recommends a compromise schedule of watering and fertilizing that works for all the orchids, so you won't have to keep separate schedules for each one. If you pot the plants in containers of similar size, try a schedule of watering once a week and fertilizing once a month. Use a high-nitrogen fertilizer (except for cymbidiums, which are fed with a low-nitrogen fertilizer from July to December). Closely watch your plants when you start this schedule. If necessary, change the potting medium to suit the watering schedule.

Orchids seldom have problems with pests and diseases. When they do, the pests are thrips, aphids, mealybugs, and scale. Orchid diseases are usually a form of root rot caused by too much water. Virus diseases are not usually a problem, unless you bring in new, diseased plants and spread the virus to your old plants. Check the orchid books for remedies. As with most good pest control, though, prevention is the key.

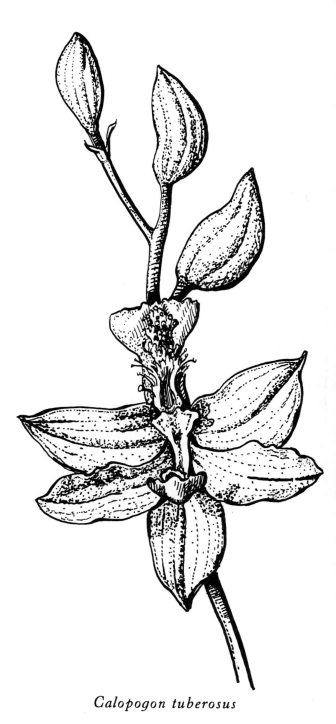

Calopogon tuberosus

Sources of Information

Books

American Orchid Society. *Handbook on Orchid Culture.* Cambridge, Mass.: American Orchid Society, 1982. A booklet covering many of the basics.

Dillon, Gordon W. *American Orchid Society, Beginner's Handbook.* Cambridge, Mass.: American Orchid Society, 1981. A fairly detailed book on most aspects of orchid growing.

Northern, Rebecca Tyson. *Home Orchid Growing.* 3rd ed. New York: Van Nostrand Reinhold Company, 1970. This book is a classic in its field, and if you have only one orchid-growing book, this should be it.

Oregon Orchid Society. *Your First Orchids and How to Grow Them.* Portland: Oregon Orchid Society, 1977. An inexpensive and pleasant way to get your feet wet.

Williams, Brian. *Orchids for Everyone.* New York: Crown Publishers, 1980. A beautiful book showing 200 orchids in color with extensive practical advice.

Williams, John G., and Williams, Andrew E. *Field Guide to Orchids of North America.* New York: Universe Books, 1983. A useful guide for looking at or photographing orchids in the wild.

Demonstration Gardens

Lahaina Orchid Exhibit
Highway 30
Lahaina, HI 96761
Over 300 varieties of orchids. Open daily.

Marie Selby Gardens
800 South Palm Drive
Sarasota, FL 33577
The center of orchid study in the United States; these people are interested in endangered species of orchids.

Nurseries

Alberts & Merkel Bros.
2210 South Federal Highway
Boynton Beach, FL 44335
Nursery open to the public.

Fennell's Orchid Jungle
26715 Southwest 157th Avenue
Homestead, FL 33031
Gardens open to the public.

Jones & Scully
2200 Northwest 33rd Avenue
Miami, FL 33142
Exhibits of orchids on the premises.

Rod McLellan Company
Acres of Orchids
1450 El Camino Real
South San Francisco, CA 94080
Large exhibit of orchids. Catalog 50 cents.

Orchids by Hausermann
P.O. Box 363
Department A
Elmhurst, IL 60126
Carries a large selection of orchids.

Fred A. Stewart Orchids
1212 East Las Tunas Drive
P.O. Box 307
San Gabriel, CA 91778
Nursery open to the public.

Organizations

For further information on orchids, join the American Orchid Society, 600 South Olive Avenue, West Palm Beach, FL 33402.

Consumer Note

A number of years ago my husband and I changed our fresh-water aquarium to a salt-water aquarium. How exciting it was to get new fish: the spectacular lion fish, the curious Humu Humu Nuku Nuku Apu Ah Ah, the graceful damsels, and the Moorish idols. They were much more interesting than the ordinary guppies and angel fish we were used to. Eventually, though, our delight changed to disappointment as one by one they starved themselves to death or contracted some exotic disease. Soon we realized that we were trying to care for *wild* creatures and that very little was known about their eating habits, diseases, and environment. They cannot even breed in captivity. To complete our disillusionment we found out that in Hawaii, where our fish had come from, natives spread household bleach in the water to stun the fish, thereby catching them easily and quickly. For every fish that ended up in someone's aquarium, hundreds of others died. Once we realized what the consequences of our fish collection were, the joy went out of the experience. We soon gave up our salt-water aquarium.

Orchids, cactuses, succulents, and other plants are often taken from the wild, usually to die in captivity. The plants, unable to reproduce, provide only a fleeting moment of pleasure for someone. And these plants represent only the tip of the iceberg; many others of their species end up withering in the sun behind some native hut, waiting to be taken to market. Taking fish, animals, and plants out of their native settings is a practice carried over from a time when there were fewer people on our planet. What may have been reasonable for hundreds is certainly not appropriate for millions. Like the leopard coat of our parents' generation that we no longer feel right owning, it no longer seems appropriate to take plants from the wild. We really don't have to anyway; we have a rich variety to choose from if we preserve our thousands of heirlooms, continue to propagate the thousands of plants already taken from the wild, and enjoy our new hybrid plants. We are gardeners blessed with choices and have no need to feel cheated.

Never collect plants from the wild unless you are rescuing a plant from the blade of a bulldozer. Be forewarned that some of our native terrestrial orchids are so difficult to grow that members of the orchid society stand up and cheer when someone gets one of them to bloom. Most orchids will not tolerate being transplanted and will not grow from seed; therefore, if you want to rescue one, get a knowledgeable person to help you. Perhaps it would be better to fight to have the plants left undisturbed. You can use the orchid guides to help you get to know native orchids. Collect pictures, not plants.

Nurseries of questionable ethics occasionally offer native, ground-dwelling orchids, such as various lady's-slippers and fringed habenarias, for sale. Avoid buying these and any other orchid that may have been collected from the wild. If you are an expert orchid grower, become involved with the American Orchid Society's program to save endangered orchids.

Never sneak orchids into the country. Besides the fact that you could end up going to jail or having to pay a whopping fine, you could introduce a new orchid pest or disease into this country.

When you start growing orchids, stay with the less expensive varieties for a while, so if you lose a few while you are learning, your cost will be minimal. Most orchids can be propagated by division, so you can save money by trading offshoots with other growers. If you do get orchids from a friend, be sure you are getting disease-free plants. If you cannot recognize most of the diseases, don't trade.

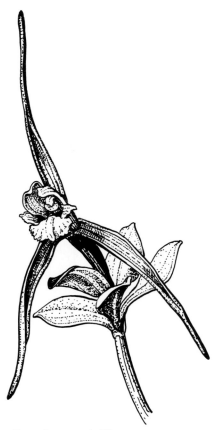

Isotria verticillata

PART THREE

PLEASURE GARDENS

Being a horticultural consultant at a party is a little like being a doctor, I imagine. Friends and acquaintances often ask what they should be doing to their gardens. Usually the questions go like this: Do I have to fertilize my lawn now? Is this the time to prune the wisteria? My plum tree is oozing sap—what should I do? In our culture, garden information gleaned from books, newspaper columns, and commercial nurseries is inevitably oriented toward what you *must do* to take care of plants. This book, while conveying many specifics about plant care, is intended as a celebration of what plants and gardening can do for you.

Instead of thinking, I have to mow the lawn now, or I have to clip the hedge before we go on a picnic today, imagine a trip to the garden as an inspiration for thinking, I wonder if there's a ripe strawberry, or I wonder if the cardinal found the nesting material I left yesterday. If the number of mandatory chores is reduced

and the garden is planned to enhance your own personal pleasure, a garden can be a source of renewal, a refuge from the world.

An Integral View of Gardening

More and more often, people are trying to integrate the different parts of their lives. They are making choices based on what is best for the whole person. This approach is needed also in the garden. Gardening is not just a lawn and a few shrubs around the house, but a whole system, a part of life. Our "concrete, microchip life" takes its toll, and viewing the yard as just one more chore that needs to be done before the weekend is over deprives you of a healthful, calming experience. Most people find renewal in nature: that trip to the mountains or to the park lifts their spirits. Yet few homeowners walk around their yards feeling more than, I had better prune that tree, or I need to water.

Gardening can be therapeutic. While gardeners have always known that, governmental studies and professional observations have now made it official: Gardening has *proven* to be of great benefit to mentally disturbed and handicapped people, seniors, prisoners, and institutionalized people. Further, schools are finding that gardening is a way to teach children about such intangibles as the seasons, the flow of time, changes in nature, and life and death.

People who have long been involved with their own gardens can speak eloquently about the feelings of well-being they get from puttering in the yard, smelling the roses, picking the tomatoes, and watching the passing seasons. Surrounded by nature, their cares melt away.

What does the typical American yard, with its large lawn, mustache of evergreen shrubs, and few trees, do for us? Well, a yard gives you distance from the neighbor's stereo; it shows you can afford some land; and it gives the children a place to play. That large lawn can also function as a barrier to rodents, fire, and insects, and it keeps dust and mud out of the house. If the trees are large, deciduous, and well placed, they can keep the house cooler in the summer.

I have no argument about the fact that these are worthwhile considerations. But let's take another look at the garden and imagine what you *could* do there: visit the vegetable garden with your child to see if the peas sown a few days ago have germinated, get out your binoculars to spy on a nest of finches, pick sun-warmed raspberries, pick a nosegay of johnny-jump-ups, or curl up to read a book under a bower of heady jasmine—maybe that's what people mean when they tell you to "smell the roses as you pass through life." If you can add these dimensions to your yard, why be content with a lawn and a few shrubs? All of us, in our own varied ways, are seeking peace of mind, fulfillment, and a feeling of integration with the natural environment. A rich source of these rewards lies just outside the window.

There is the healthful exercise to be had from gardening, and, concurrently, that wonderful feeling of actively participating in the natural scheme of life. Sharing that experience with your children can result in many rich, sun-filled hours that later on will seem to have been idyllic.

We all, regardless of our ages and levels of experience, can learn from our contact with nature. Children come to understand birth, death, and renewal in the garden, and adults as well need hands-on exposure to these cycles to remind them of what is really important. Somehow a job deadline, a bank statement, or even a serious illness in the family slips into a different perspective during an afternoon or a weekend of gardening. The new perspective encompasses both the changefulness and the stability of the natural order. You can stand in the garden and think through natural connections until you've seen the links between yourself, your own plot of land, and the Milky Way itself. There's pleasure and balance in that kind of thinking.

On a less cosmic level, consider the great fun you can have in feeding, quite literally, your other pleasures. If you're a cook, why not extend your creative touch to growing the produce you prepare in the kitchen? Do you like Italian cooking? Grow pear tomatoes, basil, and arugula. French cooking? Grow fraises des bois, flageolets, and mache. Chinese cooking? Grow bok choy, fuzzy gourds, and yard-long beans. You'll lessen your dependence on the market and give new meaning to the word *fresh*.

Is making your home comfortable and pretty your particular source of enjoyment? Why let your pleasure end at the door? Think about designing your *total* environment, cooling and heating the inside by making good landscaping decisions outside. Plant shade trees against the south wall; put in evergreen windbreaks to soften the effects of winter winds. Reserve part of your garden as a year-round source of cut flowers for the house. Create natural beauty everywhere; the only limits to your choices are the regional ones that determine the particular varieties of plants you can grow.

If you love animals or butterflies or certain kinds of plants, such as cactuses or succulents, or if you would like to teach your children about these things, design your yard to support those species and watch them flourish. Plants give us a sense of our own place in the natural world. The gardens in Part Three are examples of ways your yard can be a source of joy.

If you give up the typical American habit of trying to dominate nature and begin to think about living with nature—as an active part of it— you'll come up with ways of designing your yard to reflect and enhance what you love. Your garden will be a source of joy and understanding and, ultimately, a place to feel at home and tranquil. Feel like going to bed? Taking a pill? Calling a therapist? Try rolling up your sleeves and doing some gardening instead.

Ficus carica

Chapter 9
The Gourmet Garden

Every week twenty years ago I tuned in to Julia Child's television program, "The French Chef." With great enthusiasm I followed her lead and made quiche, ratatouille, salade nicoise, crepes, and numerous other goodies. I, like many Americans, was being awakened to a whole new way of cooking and eating. Our gastronomy changed dramatically as a consequence of several factors: Julia's program and cookbooks, an upswing in our economy and the resulting societal changes, and increased education and travel. In the last two decades the improvements in cooking skills and the wide availability of exotic ingredients have changed the American palate. Twenty years ago only the very sophisticated or well-traveled person had heard of kiwis, tacos, pesto, shallots, and chutney. Now most people have.

If we take stock of gastronomy in the mid-1980s, we are led to the conclusion that eating more home-grown fruits and vegetables is the order. For instance, we are becoming more health conscious and have begun to cut back on salt, butter, and calories. We suspect there are unsafe additives and pesticides in our produce. If we grow our own food, we will ingest fewer chemicals. If we eat more fruits and vegetables, we have more roughage in our diets—the nutritionists tell us that is healthful.

Since the oil crisis, food prices have skyrocketed, and the high price of food has become an issue. It is expensive to eat well. Of particular interest to the gourmet cook is the fact that even though there is a huge selection of fruits and vegetables at the market, the quality is slipping. The hybridization of fruits and vegetables to make them as firm as cardboard for machine picking and packing and the early harvesting of unripe produce to ensure it withstands long-distance shipping have resulted in an ever-increasing choice of beautiful but tasteless produce: the nickel apple that costs a quarter and tastes like nothing.

Most home-grown produce is far superior to what you can buy. It's fresher and usually more succulent, and that is because it can be picked at its peak. However, several caveats are in order here. Some of the worst produce I have eaten has come from my garden. Cucumbers must be picked when they are young; they develop tough seeds as they mature. Pears that are allowed to ripen on the tree get grainy. Overripe melons are soft and mushy. The point I am making is that growing your own produce is only half of the answer to eating well; in addition, you must learn when each vegetable and fruit is at its peak. To do that, you must be diligent. Experiment: try picking at different times and see at which stage individual vegetables and fruits are most appealing to you.

You must have reasonable expectations for your home-grown produce. Some edibles that you buy from the grocery store can't be duplicated at home. For instance, commercially produced 'Thompson Seedless' grapes are larger and sweeter than those grown at home. Farmers spray a plant hormone, gibberellic acid, on the grapes to make them large, and they girdle the stems of the vines to prevent the sugars from migrating to the roots. Most homeowners do neither. Also, different soils and climates produce different tastes. My tomatoes in California have never had as much tomato flavor as those from my New England garden; and my California-grown onions are very hot, even when I plant the sweetest, mildest varieties. Through experimentation and adventurous selection of varieties you will develop a list of superior edibles for your own garden and table.

In order to learn which varieties of fruits and vegetables do well in your area, frequent farmers' and gourmet produce markets. If the produce is not labeled with the name of its variety, ask the produce manager or the farmer who grew it what it is. Keep a record of the varieties you prefer so that when winter bare-root planting season comes or when it is time to order seeds in the spring, you will know which varieties are your favorites. Learning about the different varieties will help you avoid the problem I so often see at the nursery: people standing in front of an array of bare-root fruit trees or at the seed racks scratching their heads, with no idea which varieties to choose.

Let's face it, many of us who enjoy gourmet cooking have a bit of the showoff in us, and I've noticed that it is getting harder to stay one up on everyone. Ten years ago I could go to a meeting of rare-fruit growers and come home to wow everyone with an exotic fruit—a kiwi, for example. Today everyone yawns. If you want to be out in front now, you must join the next gourmet frontier: home-grown produce. Home-grown corn, new potatoes, petits pois, as well as more unusual varieties such as adzuki beans, water chestnuts, quince, and loganberries, can be grown at home to produce rave reviews at the table.

A home vegetable garden can dramatically enrich your cuisine, and in most cases the unusual edibles are no harder to grow than common fruits and vegetables. As a rule, you must purchase the unusual edibles by mail or from specialty nurseries.

Gourmet Plants for the Outdoor Garden

I recommend the following plants and seeds for a beginning gourmet gardener; only a few of them are available in grocery stores, and all will enrich your table fare.

Avocados. 'Mexicola' avocados are my favorite; they taste like melted cashews. They are little and soft skinned, which is probably why they aren't found in grocery stores. In addition, if you have a greenhouse or live in a warm climate, you can try the exciting, new dwarf avocado, 'Whitsell'. It is a good, green-skinned avocado that growers have spent years producing. Pacific Tree Farms, 4301 Lynwood Drive, Chula Vista, CA 92010, is one of the first nurseries to carry this 'Hass'-type avocado.

Bamboo. Fresh bamboo shoots are sweet and succulent. Varieties that are easily grown in many parts of this country produce shoots in the spring or fall.

Beets. Yellow beets have made cooking with beets more versatile because, unlike red beets, they do not "bleed" into soups, stir-fried dishes, salads, and stews.

Corn. Hopi blue corn is easy to grow, makes incredible cornbread and tamales, and is almost never available at the grocery store.

Cucumbers. Armenian cucumbers have a wonderful cucumber taste and don't cause the burps that standard cucumbers give some people. My Indian friend says that they also make the best raita.

Elderberries. Elderberries make superb pies, jam, and wine but are rarely used for such.

Garlic. Elephant garlic is much easier to peel, and, while not as pungent as ordinary garlic, the large cloves are mild and tasty.

Ginger. Ginger that is grown outside in the summer and brought inside when it gets cold not only produces flavorful rhizomes but also tasty green shoots for use in salads and stir-fried dishes.

Heirloom fruits. Fruits that will elicit comments from your guests are 'Cox's Pippin', an antique apple from England; currants in the form of jelly; and quinces, which make the best baked "apples" you've ever tasted.

Herbs. Fresh herbs such as thyme, red basil, sage, pineapple mint, chervil, savory, and anise lend much more aroma and flavor to cooking than their dried equivalents and are at their best when picked only minutes before you use them.

Hops. Hops are easily grown, and they produce edible shoots every spring that are similar to asparagus. They can be cooked and served the same way as asparagus.

Nuts. There are new varieties of nuts available, especially the self-pollinating, pink-flowered, dwarf 'Garden Prince' almond. The North American Nut Growers Association is currently trying to develop a hardy pecan variety and a disease-resistant chestnut.

Oranges. 'Tarocco' oranges, sometimes called raspberry, or blood, oranges, have red, tangy juice that will make you yawn at ordinary orange juice.

Peaches. 'Indian Blood' peaches are deep red inside. Can them or make a beautiful red jam with them.

Salad greens. Flavorful greens such as sorrel, mache (corn salad), salad burnet, orach, and rocket (arugula) are flavorful additions to humdrum salads.

Fresh salad greens make a dramatic addition to your table fare. They grow well in containers and are beautiful in any garden.

Strawberries. Alpine strawberries are so delicate that they barely survive the trip from garden to table, much less by truck to store to home. Their fragrance alone is worth the experience of growing them.

Zucchini. Golden zucchini is a tasty and colorful addition to omelets, salads, and soups.

Gourmet Plants for the Greenhouse

Following is a list of delightful edibles that can be grown in a greenhouse.

Banana. Home-grown bananas are small but have much more flavor than those purchased at the store, and the leaves are wonderful to steam vegetables in: they impart a fragrance to the food. 'Enano Gigante' dwarf bananas are particularly well suited to greenhouse growing.

Cherimoyas. Succulent, creamy fruits that currently sell at $8 to $10 per pound and are considered one of the finest fruits in the world. They grow on large shrubs that are suitable for greenhouse growing, though the flowers will need to be hand-pollinated. 'Mariella' is a good variety to try.

Vanilla. Pods grow on an orchid vine that can be grown in the greenhouse. They are difficult orchids to grow but are a challenge for the experienced gardener and worth the effort.

Ethnic Cooking

Many ingredients for the different ethnic cuisines are easy-to-grow herbs and annual vegetables that can be grown in most parts of the country. Related varieties, such as string beans and the French haricots verts, are grown the same way their American cousins are; and vegetables such as sorrel, garland chrysanthemum, and mache are generally very easy to grow. To give you an idea of what is feasible in your garden, look over the following list.

Oriental Ingredients You Can Grow

Amaranth (pot herb). A hot to bland, depending on the variety, spinach-type vegetable. Use it in soups and stir-fried dishes, or steam it by itself.

Bitter melon (vegetable). A slightly bitter summer-squash-like vegetable. It can be stuffed with pork and herbs or used in stir-fried dishes or steamed like spinach.

Burdock, gobo (root vegetable). The leaves are eaten the way spinach is. The root, which is somewhat pungent, can be used as a root vegetable: steamed, stir fried, and in soups.

Chinese cabbage. A mild-tasting, sweet, succulent cabbage used in Chinese soups, stir-fried dishes, salads, and pickling.

Chinese okra. A sweet zucchinilike vegetable that can be eaten raw in salads. It can be stir fried, deep fried, simmered, or stuffed.

Chinese parsley (cilantro). A zesty herb that is used in many vegetable and meat dishes.

Daikon (radish). Grate and serve raw in Japanese cuisine, stir fry with shellfish, and pickle for Chinese cuisine.

Daylilies (golden needles). The buds of the daylily are sweet, tasty additions to Chinese soups and meat and vegetable dishes.

Fuzzy gourd (vegetable). A sweet summer-squash-like vegetable that can be steamed or used in stir-fried dishes and soups.

Garland chrysanthemum, shungiku (pot herb). A fragrant green that is used in soups and stir-fried dishes or steamed like spinach.

Sesame. A versatile plant that provides leaves, which can be cooked as a vegetable, and seeds, which add a characteristic nutty flavor to salads, stir-fried dishes, and vegetable dishes.

Yard-long beans. Tasty, very long string beans that are used in stir-fried dishes. They are fabulous as a dry-braised dish and can be used wherever string beans are.

Good sources of Oriental seeds are Redwood City Seed Company and Shepherd's Garden Seeds. The addresses of these companies are given at the end of this chapter.

French Ingredients You Can Grow

Alpine strawberries. The most delicate and aromatic of all strawberries. These small, wildlike strawberries will make any fruit salad or tart a special occasion.

Celeriac (root vegetable). A root vegetable with a sweet celery taste. Superb served julienne sliced in a remoulade and in salads and cooked dishes.

Chervil (herb). A mild herb that adds a subtle richness to egg dishes, seafood, and salads.

Courgettes (squash). This tender summer squash is versatile; it is enhanced by many different sauces and cooking techniques.

Haricots verts (beans). Tender, pencil thin, string beans that are great just by themselves or in soups, salads, and vegetable dishes.

Mache, corn salad

Mache (corn salad). A tender, subtle-tasting salad green.

Petits pois (peas). These are the small, incredibly sweet peas that make the regular varieties unacceptable by comparison.

Roquette (salad green). A rich salad green that adds a zesty flavor to bland greens.

Shallot. A relative of onion and garlic, the shallot has inherited the best of both. Useful where onion and garlic are featured.

Sorrel (pot herb). A slightly sour, succulent green that is fabulous in salads and soups.

Good sources of French seeds are Epicure Seeds Ltd., Le Marche Seeds International, and Shepherd's Garden Seeds. The addresses of these companies are given at the end of this chapter.

Mexican Ingredients You Can Grow

Chayote (vegetable). A versatile squashlike vegetable that adds a sweet, nutty flavor to soups and stews and is beautiful just steamed by itself.

Chilies. These peppers add authority to Mexican cuisine, and the fresh varieties add a perfume that dried chilies only hint at.

Cilantro (herb). A commonly used herb that tastes similar to parsley.

Jicama (vegetable). A very sweet, watery, crisp vegetable. It can be sliced into salads to add extra crispness and into soups and stews.

Nopales (cactus pads). Sliced cactus pads are an unusual vegetable; they are sweet and similar to string beans in taste. They can be steamed and fried and are sometimes smothered in sauces.

Tomatillo (vegetable). A close relative of the tomato, this tasty, small, green globe gives a richness to green salsa and is a treat fried, stewed, and in soups.

Good sources of Mexican seeds are Redwood City Seed Company and Shepherd's Garden Seeds. The addresses of these companies are given at the end of this chapter.

Indian Ingredients You Can Grow

Bitter melon (vegetable). A slightly bitter, tasty, squashlike vegetable you can use in dishes that feature its unusual taste.

Chilies. Fresh chili peppers give bite and the characteristic hotness to Indian food. Fresh chilies can be grated or chopped finely and used in chutneys, curries, soups, and pickles.

'Gypsy' peppers are outstanding—sweet, crisp, and thin-walled.

Cilantro (herb). A parsleylike herb that is dried and used in chutneys, curries, rice, and vegetable dishes. Use it fresh as a flavoring and garnish. You cannot do very much authentic Indian cooking without it.

Ginger. A succulent rhizome that adds a heady aroma and hotness to many Indian dishes, including curries, rice and lentil dishes, sweets, and pickles.

Fenugreek (herb). This herb is used fresh whenever possible. It is added to chutneys and spice tea and is used as a garnish.

Saffron (spice). A pungent, orange-colored spice obtained from the saffron crocus. It is used in Indian cooking to add an exciting taste to rice, curries, and sweets.

A good source of Indian seeds is Redwood City Seed Company, whose address is given at the end of this chapter.

An Italian Gourmet Vegetable Garden

When people think of Italian cuisine, they usually think of pizza, spaghetti, and other pasta dishes. While they are certainly Italian, those dishes make up only a small part of Italian cuisine. To my mind, Italian cuisine is marinated vegetables (bright red peppers, sweet onions, and mushrooms bathed in olive oil, vinegar, and herbs), eggplant parmigiana, deep-fried cardoon (a close relative of the artichoke), peas with prosciutto, and bagna cauda (raw vegetables dipped in hot butter and olive oil flavored with garlic and anchovies). It is antipasto, minestrone, pesto (a sauce of pureed fresh basil, olive oil, and garlic), and colorful salads with magenta chicories called radicchio and bright green endive and arugula. It was my good fortune to enjoy these dishes in Italy, and because most of these dishes are filled with fresh herbs and unusually succulent and colorful vegetables, I found that the only way to duplicate many of the taste sensations I had experienced was to grow some of the vegetables and herbs myself.

To really do justice to most ethnic cuisines, you need produce that is usually either not available in American grocery stores or, if it is available, is exorbitantly expensive; and Italian cuisine, I found, is no exception. It requires fresh basil, cilantro, and dill, for instance, and fresh fava beans, white Italian eggplant, 'Romanesco' broccoli with its sculptured conical heads and lively taste, scorzonera and ravanello (large brown and white radishes), squash blossoms, radicchio (red and striped chicories), and finnochio (sweet fennel). These are all outstanding vegetables that are seldom seen in this country, except in home vegetable gardens or in the fanciest restaurants.

If you want to experience some of Italy's best cuisine, put in a vegetable garden similar to the one illustrated here; it is based on the garden of Vicki Sebastiani, who is married to Sam Sebastiani, the president of Sebastiani Vineyards. Vicki has been a vegetable gardener since she was four years old and is often called upon to entertain hundreds of people and to contribute recipes to the winery's newsletter. Vicki's interest in vegetable gardening has grown to prodigious proportions. Last summer her garden included one hundred varieties of vegetables and herbs, most of them Italian. There were red, yellow, and white varieties of Italian tomatoes, white eggplant, Italian yellow and light green zucchini, giant cauliflower, variegated chicory, long beans, spaghetti squash, horseradish, and scarlet runner beans. Red and white flowers were interspersed among the vegetables and herbs.

Planning and Preparation

Vicki offers the following information for the aspiring Italian gourmet vegetable gardener. Most of the superior, authentic varieties of vegetable seeds are not available at nurseries. You must order them by mail early in the spring, or, if you are as fortunate as Vicki, get them in Italy when you visit there. She ordered most of her seeds from Gurney Seed and Nursery Company and W. Atlee Burpee Company. Some of the varieties that she bought in Italy can be purchased from DeGiorgi Company, Epicure Seeds, and Shepherd's Garden Seeds (the addresses of these companies are given at the end of this chapter). Each company carries a number of Italian vegetable and herb

Right Vicki Sebastiani grows 'Romanesco' broccoli in her Italian vegetable garden.

seeds. You will not, however, be able to buy seeds for some of the vegetables you see on the list. They are a challenge. Perhaps if you have Italian friends or neighbors, they will share some of their open-pollinated varieties with you. Perhaps you can visit Italy or find a seed source there.

Once you have gotten the seeds, choose a sunny, well-drained garden area and add large amounts of organic matter. Start the tomatoes, peppers, eggplants, squashes, and cantaloupes indoors early in the spring so that you can transplant them into the garden after all chance of frost has passed. When your soil starts to warm up in the spring, you can plant the seeds of some of the early vegetables, such as lettuce, peas, carrots, spinach, radishes, turnips, kohl-rabies, cauliflower, broccoli, chicory, endive, fennel, and nasturtiums. Once the weather has completely warmed up, with no possibility of frost, you can plant the seeds of beans, dill, corn, and okra and transplant the tender plants that you started weeks before. Consult local authorities for exact dates for planting your garden. The varieties suggested in this garden have the same cultural requirements—water, fertilizer, and pest control, if any—as your usual varieties.

Following is a list of vegetables and herbs that is keyed to the layout of a variation of the Sebastiani gourmet garden. Notice that not all the vegetables and herbs are Italian; many are American. Vicki's garden is a very ambitious project and too large for the average family. so scale yours down to a more manageable size. Not all the plants were grown in the same season. Some are spring crops; others are summer and fall crops. The numbers preceding the plants are keyed to the diagram on page 141. Following the plant name there is often, in brackets, the name of a seed company. Those companies are either where Vicki obtained her seeds or where I have located the seeds or seeds of a very similar variety. Where there is no company name, Vicki obtained the seeds either in Italy or from local nurseries. Addresses of the seed companies are given at the end of this chapter.

1. Basil [Burpee]
2. Cavolfiore Precocissimo di Jesi (Italian white cauliflower)
3. Cavolfiore, 'Grodan' (Italian snow white cauliflower)
4. Cavolbroccolo d'Albenga, 'Bronzino' (spear-shaped Italian broccoli)
5. Cavolfiore di Sicilia, Catanese (Italian red cauliflower)
6. Cavolbroccolo, 'Romanesco' (Italian light green, small-speared broccoli) [Epicure, Seeds Blum]
7. Kohlrabi, 'Grand Duke' [Gurney's, Burpee]
8. Kohlrabi, 'Early Purple' Vienna [Gurney's, Burpee]
9. Pepper, 'Sweet Bell'
10. Pepper, 'Big Jim New Mex' [Gurney's]
11. Pepper, 'Spartan Garnet' [Gurney's]
12. Pepper, 'Fresno Chili Grande' [Gurney's]
13. Pepper, pepperoncini [Gurney's]
14. Pepper, jalapeno [Gurney's, Burpee]
15. Pepper, 'Santa Fe Grande' [Gurney's]
16. Alchechenge (small, Italian yellow pear tomato)
17. Tomato, 'Golden Boy' [Gurney's]
18. Tomato, 'Golden Delight' [Gurney's Early Yellow]
19. Tomato, 'Yellow Pear' [Gurney's, DeGiorgi]
20. Tomato, 'White Beauty' [Gurney's]
21. Tomato, 'Pink Delight' [Gurney's]
22. Tomato, 'Beefmaster' [Gurney's]
23. Okra, 'Clemson Spineless' [Gurney's]
24. Okra, red [Gurney's, DeGiorgi]
25. Squash, 'Golden Zucchini' [Burpee]
26. Squash, 'White Patty Pan' [Burpee, DeGiorgi]
27. Squash, 'Green Patty Pan' [Gurney's]
28. Squash, 'Gold Zucchini' [Gurney's]
29. Squash, Zucchetta Goldzinni (Italian yellow zucchini)

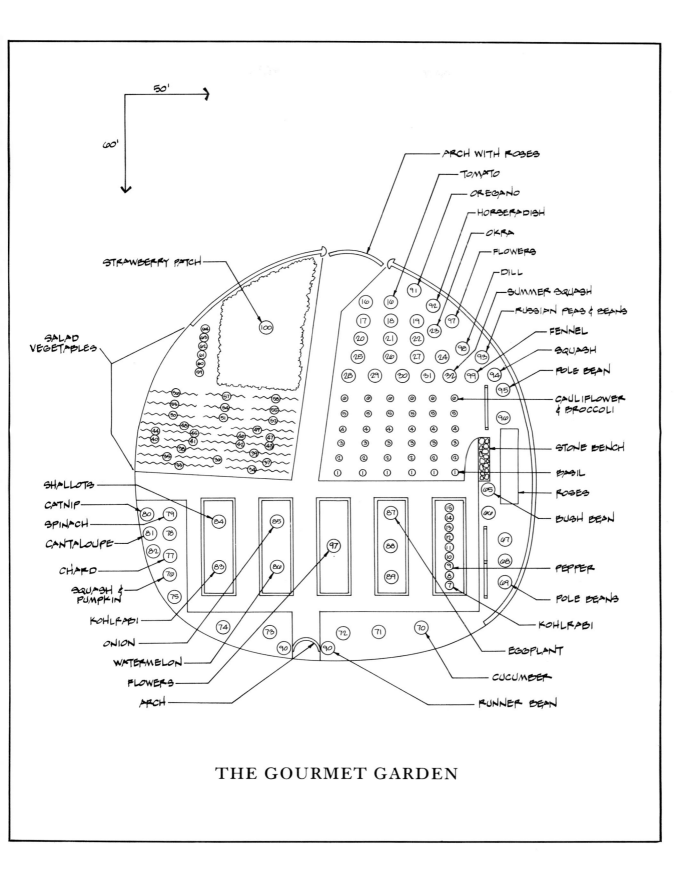

THE GOURMET GARDEN

30. Squash, Zucchetta Bianca Della Virginia (Italian light green zucchini)
31. Squash, 'Rich Green Zucchini' [Burpee]
32. Squash, 'Petite Crookneck' [Gurney's]
33. Nasturtium [Burpee]
34. Radish, 'Champion O' Giants'
35. Ravanello (Italian 24-inch white radish)
36. Radish, daikon [Gurney's, Burpee]
37. Scorzonera (24-inch brown radish, salsify) [DeGiorgi]
38. Sugar pea, 'Dwarf White' [Gurney's]
39. Turnip, 'Sweet White' [Gurney's]
40. Spinach, 'Iron Duke' [Gurney's]
41. Cicoria Invernale
42. Cicoria Palla di Fuoco Rossa
43. Cicoria, red variegated
44. Lettuce, green curled [Burpee]
45. Lettuce, 'Dark Green Boston' [Burpee]
46. Lettuce, 'Sweetie Leaf' [Gurney's]
47. Lettuce, 'Buttercrunch' [Gurney's]
48. Endive, 'Green Curled' [Burpee]
49. Carrot, 'Nantes Half Long' [Burpee]
50. Cicoria (Italian butter lettuce)
51. Cicoria Endivia (Italian curly endive)
52. Arugula (roquette, or rocket) [Shepherd's, Epicure]
53. Valeriana (Italian leaf lettuce)
54. Lattughino (Italian small-leaf lettuce)
55. Cicoria Rossadi Treviso (Italian red tight endive) [Shepherd's, Epicure]
56. Misticanza (mixed Italian lettuces)
57. Bieta Green (Italian leaf lettuce)
58. Lettuga (Italian red lettuce)
59. Prezzemolo (Italian parsley) [Epicure]
60. Parsley, single [Burpee]
61. Parsley, 'Extra-Curled Dwarf' [Burpee]
62. Parsley, 'Moss Curled'
63. Dandelion, thick-leaved
64. Dandelion, French
65. Bean, 'Bush Blue Lake' [Burpee]
66. Bean, 'Bush Yellow' [Burpee]
67. Experimental pole bean (entirely edible)
68. Bean, Fagiolo Rampicante (Italian green pole bean that can grow to 3 feet in length)
69. Bean, Fagiolo Rampicante Borlotto (Italian purple pole bean)
70. Cucumber, Citriolo Bianco Lunghissimo (Italian white cucumber)
71. Cucumber, 'West India Gherkin' [Burpee]
72. Cucumber, 'White Wonder'
73. Squash, cucuzzi (Italian edible gourd) [DeGiorgi]
74. Squash, 'Jumbo Pink Banana'
75. Squash, spaghetti [DeGiorgi, Burpee]
76. Pumpkin, 'Jack-O'-Lantern'
77. Bieta (Italian white chard)
78. Bieta Rosse (Italian red chard)
79. Spinach, New Zealand [DeGiorgi]
80. Catnip (for "Mouser," the cat) [Burpee]
81. Cantaloupe, 'Ambrosia' [Burpee]
82. Cantaloupe, 'Gospe's French'
83. Kohlrabi, 'Early White Vienna' [Gurney's, Burpee]
84. Shallots
85. Cippola (Italian white giant onion) [Epicure]
86. Watermelon, 'Petite Sweet' [Gurney's]
87. Melanzana bianca ovale (white Italian eggplant) [Seeds Blum]
88. Eggplant, 'Black Beauty'
89. Eggplant, Japanese
90. Scarlet runner beans [Seeds Blum]
91. Oregano
92. Horseradish
93. Russian peas and beans
94. Squash, 'Butter Bush' [Burpee]
95. Beans, 'Roma II' [Shepherd's]
96. Beans, 'Romano'
97. Flowers
98. Dill
99. Fennel
100. Strawberry patch

Clockwise from left Elwin Meader has been instrumental in introducing a number of superior vegetables and fruits to this country. Here he stands at his New Hampshire home with his hardy kiwi vine, which is able to stand temperatures as low as 25 degrees below zero F. The hardy kiwi, *Actinidia arguta,* is available from Michael McConkey, Edible Landscaping Nursery, Route 2, Box 343A, Afton, VA 22920.

The fruit of the hardy kiwi, shown in this close-up photograph, tastes just like its larger cousin that is available in the grocery store, but its skin is green and smooth; instead of peeling the fruit, you pop it into your mouth as you would a cherry.

Peter Chan of Portland, Oregon, is famous for his vegetable garden—it contains many Chinese varieties. Here he is examining a fuzzy gourd vine that grows much like cucumber vines do.

Sources of Information

Books

Harrington, Geri. *Grow Your Own Chinese Vegetables*. New York: Collier Books, 1978. Definitely the complete word on how to grow Oriental vegetables and herbs in this country.

James, Theodore, Jr. *The Gourmet Garden*. New York: E.P. Dutton, 1983. Extensive information on many superior types and varieties of vegetables and fruits.

Jeavons, John, and Leler, Robin. *The Seed Finder*. Willits, Calif.: Jeavons-Leler, 1983. The key to growing superior vegetables is knowing where to get the seeds. The authors have done a service to gardeners by providing information on where to get many of the best vegetable seed varieties.

Morash, Marian. *The Victory Garden Cookbook*. New York: Alfred A. Knopf, 1982. My favorite vegetable cookbook.

Organic Gardening and Farming editorial staff. *Gourmet Gardening*. Edited by Anne Moyer Halpin. Emmaus, Pa.: Rodale Press, 1978. Specific information on how to grow many unusual and superior vegetables.

Sunset Books editorial staff. *Sunset Italian Cookbook*. Menlo Park, Calif.: Lane Publishing Co., 1974. A good basic Italian cookbook.

Waters, Alice. *Chez Panisse Menu Cookbook*. New York: Random House, 1982. An inspiring cookbook by an author who feels that fresh, superior, home-grown produce is the starting point for outstanding cuisine.

Demonstration Gardens

The Boonville Hotel
Boonville, CA 95415
This is really a restaurant (although it may be a hotel in the future) that serves vegetables from the garden. You can see many outstanding varieties growing there and taste some in the restaurant.

Chicago Botanical Garden
Lake Cook Road
Glencoe, IL 60022
The botanical garden is opening a demonstration food garden and will start giving demonstrations and cooking classes.

Nurseries

W. Atlee Burpee Company
Warminster, PA 18974
Burpee has a wide selection of vegetable seeds for the home gardener.

DeGiorgi Company
Council Bluffs, IA 51502
This nursery imports seeds of many of the Italian vegetables as well as many of the standard varieties.

Epicure Seeds Ltd.
P.O. Box 450
Brewster, NY 10509
This seed company specializes in European seeds.

Gurney's Seed & Nursery Company
Yankton, SD 57079
Gurney's has a large collection of unusual vegetable varieties.

Le Marche Seeds International
P.O. Box 566
Dixon, CA 95620
This company specializes in French and heirloom vegetable seeds.

Redwood City Seed Company
P.O. Box 361
Redwood City, CA 94064
This company carries many varieties of Oriental, Mexican, Indian, and open-pollinated vegetable seeds.

Seeds Blum
Idaho City Stage
Boise, ID 83707
This company specializes in open-pollinated seeds that often are old-time varieties. Many are similar to some of the Italian varieties, and some are the actual Italian varieties themselves.

Shepherd's Garden Seeds
7389 West Zayante Road
Felton, CA 95018
A gourmet seed company specializing in European varieties.

Chapter 10
The Child's Garden

My introduction to gardening was a delightful one. When I was four or five years old, my father gave me my own patch of soil under an ancient apple tree. It was near his vegetable garden, close enough so that we could chat and wonder together. In my plot I planted his extra seeds; I watered everything in sight, moved his extra strawberry runners, and watched marigolds and tomato plants sprout. While I sometimes helped him pick beans, plant corn, and mine for potatoes, I seemed to enjoy most moving plants around in my own garden. I treated my garden much like I treated my doll house: as something that needed constant rearranging. I seldom produced anything, and most of my plants died because they were weary from being moved. Nevertheless, I have wonderful memories of "gardening" with my father. Looking back on that experience, I can see what an ideal environment it was for learning. There were never any gardening dicta. I

wasn't told, "You must not move your carrots." Instead, I moved my carrots and discovered that, instead of straight, succulent carrots, I got "many-gnarled things," multipointed corkscrews! I proved, to my satisfaction, at least, that plants don't like to be moved. In addition to learning a few specifics, I also learned about the birth of spring, the fullness of life in the summer, and the dying in the fall. Abstract principles became real.

My garden experience was not only experimental; if I asked specific questions, I usually got answers. And, most often, not answers phrased as facts, but more as sharing wonders. For example, I remember asking my father why he was spreading ashes from the fireplace in the garden. Instead of being told that ashes contain potash that can be used by the plants, I remember a discussion of how nature recycles everything. We speculated on where the smoke went and what happened to the heat and what was left that the corn could use. Instead of a teacher-pupil relationship, we shared in the experience of questioning. We wondered why mint had square stems and where our robins went in the winter. We commiserated with one another when the blue jays dug up our newly planted corn or when the cutworms ate to the ground the baby squash plants. We ate sun-warmed tomatoes together and enjoyed being among living things. I did not learn when or how deep to plant corn seeds or many other practical things; those I had to look up later in a book. What I learned was much more valuable —love for the garden and a respectful awe of nature.

I've shared my own childhood gardening experience because it seems the best way to illustrate that a child's garden will be the most enriching experience if it is filled with sharing and wonder, rather than with lists of "thou shalts" and "thou shalt nots." If my father had chided me about moving my plants around or made me spend hours weeding and raking, my feelings about gardening would probably be quite different from what they are. If my father had felt obliged to "teach" me gardening, he probably wouldn't have enjoyed having me in the garden as much as he did. Instead, our gardening was a pleasure for both of us.

Shared moments in the garden with children are rewarding, but in stressing only time in the garden itself, you might overlook other ways to experience nature. The growing experience can be felt in many ways. You can put out bird food in the winter during a storm or bring in the pussy willow as a celebration of spring or let a sweet potato or carrot that has started to sprout grow on the windowsill. Grow your own bean sprouts and let the children help. Instead of their just playing house under the card table, maybe they could create a greenhouse with a few house plants. Gardens are not isolated expressions of nature; they are an integral part.

I think children should have a garden experience so that they can grow up appreciating that they are part of the web of nature, not beings outside of it. And what a joy if they can experience it with a wonder that will stay with them all of their lives. Further, it seems important for children to grow up knowing that food does not originate at the corner market, but is a gift from the earth that they can participate in.

Getting Children Started in the Garden

Here are a few ideas to help you and your children find pleasure in the garden. If at all possible, get the book *Growing Up Green* (listed at the end of this chapter). It captures the essence of the whole experience, and I can't recommend it highly enough. If you have the space, give your child a growing area. It does not have to be a garden; it can be as simple as a planter box or a potato in a bucket of compost.

Help them send for their own seed catalogs and seeds. Children love to get mail, and receiving their seeds by mail is often half the fun. In addition, you may want to become involved with the local 4-H, a particularly good organization for older children that will also be a source of information for you if you are a beginning gardener. Another way to bring the love of gardening to your children is to try to get the school interested in a gardening program. You may want to volunteer your help.

If you are able to give your children garden space, start with plants that grow quickly and easily. Include at least a few edible plants in the project because they seem to provide more interest for children than flowers do. It certainly isn't necessary for the child to produce bushels of tomatoes or potatoes in order to enjoy gardening—remember my "moving" garden—however, it seems to help to guide them in a successful and fruitful direction because children usually get excited by producing something. My eight-year-old niece started gardening in Florida with strawberry plants that already had little, immature straw-

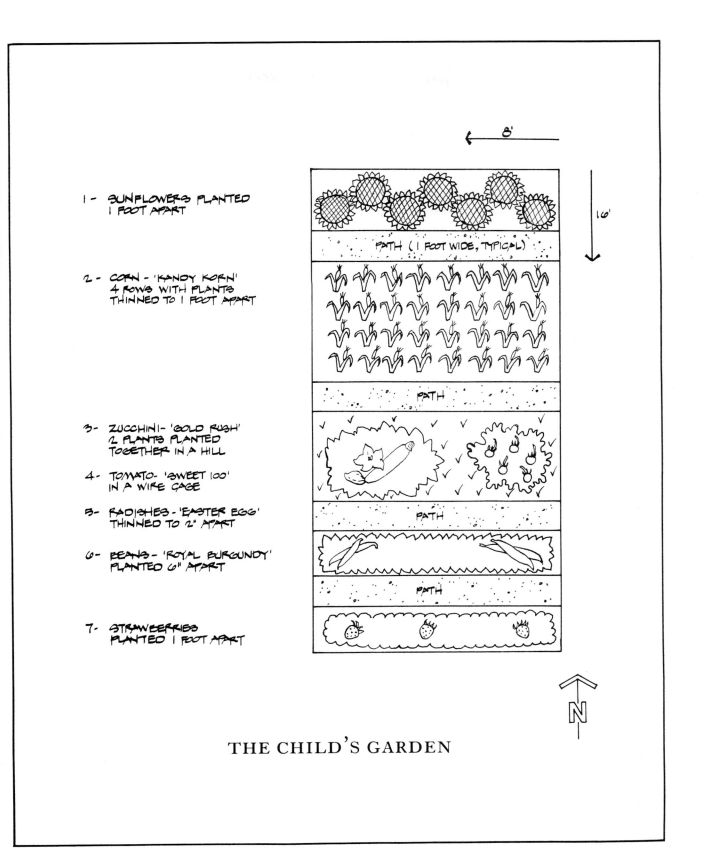

1 – SUNFLOWERS PLANTED 1 FOOT APART

2 – CORN – 'KANDY KORN' 4 ROWS WITH PLANTS THINNED TO 1 FOOT APART

3 – ZUCCHINI – 'GOLD RUSH' 2 PLANTS PLANTED TOGETHER IN A HILL

4 – TOMATO – 'SWEET 100' IN A WIRE CAGE

5 – RADISHES – 'EASTER EGG' THINNED TO 2" APART

6 – BEANS – 'ROYAL BURGUNDY' PLANTED 6" APART

7 – STRAWBERRIES PLANTED 1 FOOT APART

8'

16'

N

THE CHILD'S GARDEN

berries on them. Because it was her first taste of gardening, the almost-instant return of ripe strawberries got her involved at the outset. We also planted two vegetables that usually do very well in Florida: tomatoes and sweet potatoes. Weeks later, when the tomatoes began to produce, she had already been "hooked." The sweet potatoes didn't produce worth a darn, but, then, that's gardening. It's not always a success, and that's part of the process too.

As you and your children are gardening together, not only can you share the wonder of nature, in addition, you have an opportunity to help stop the spread of insect phobias. Children learn by example, and before they grow up, they will see hundreds of commercials on television for insecticides, in which hysterical people run from bugs. To counteract that knee-jerk reaction, which accounts for a great deal of unnecessary pesticide usage and exposure, you can marvel at the spider in your closet and put it outside, instead of routinely clobbering it with the newspaper. I know that is difficult for many folks. Maybe all you can do is to say to your child, "I wish I didn't feel like killing the spider." That would, at least, acknowledge that your reaction to kill the spider is irrational.

It doesn't take a lot to change attitudes. One day I was visiting a neighbor whose children, aged seven, nine, and ten, were swimming in the pool. A very large stag beetle, flying near the surface of the water, was hit by a wave and fell in. The children immediately scrambled out of the pool in a panic, and their mother, who is afraid of insects, was trying to figure out how to get it out of the pool. With a dramatic flair, I reached down gently and allowed the beetle to climb on my hand, lifted it out of the pool, and put it on the deck. You should have seen everyone's face; it was as though I had bearded the lion in its den. As the beetle started to amble off, fear turned to fascination. I then went home and brought back my field guide to insects and showed the children how to look it up. As a result, these three children

became so interested in insects that they now occasionally show up at my house bearing "bugs" in a jar, wanting me to help identify them.

It seems to me that the best way you can give your children the gift of gardening is to enjoy it with them. Give them a supportive environment for their gardening experience rather than a list of how-to's. As Alice Skelsey and Gloria Huckaby say in their book, *Growing Up Green,* "Gardening is caught, not taught."

Planning and Preparation

Through the years, as a child and as an adult, certain aspects of gardening have tickled my soul. I have listed some of them here as a starting place for novice gardeners of any age.

Growing vegetables can be as simple as planting a dozen crocus bulbs in a container or as involving as planting a large vegetable garden. If your space and time are very limited, start small. A simple garden can be a large plastic bag of potting soil placed in full sun on a patio. Slit the bag, poke a few holes in the bottom, and put the bag where it won't stain the patio. Plant a few potatoes, two petunia plants, a cherry tomato, or a zucchini plant. Have your child water it occasionally and fertilize it once a month; then enjoy the harvest. Or you can order a packet of wildflower seeds from a catalog and sprinkle them over a small patch of prepared soil, making sure they stay moist for a few weeks. Let them grow while you and your children wonder which flowers will appear. Another simple but rewarding project is to buy a few dozen tulip bulbs in the fall and help your young child plant them. Little effort, much reward.

If you can, however, set aside a small piece of ground for your child's vegetable garden; then simply plant some or all of the annual vegetables and herbs listed below. These plants are, I think, a good place to start with children. There is nothing exclusively childish about the following list; it is a great place to start for any gardener, no matter the age and skill. The list contains particular vegetables and specific varieties that I personally find rewarding and interesting to grow. I am confident that it holds things of fascination for children, and for the child in all of us. You will notice that I recommend a number of vegetables and fruits that are unusual colors. Growing unusual vegetables often adds another element of wonder and excitement to gardening.

An alternative that you may find appealing is to get an entire children's garden that has already been preselected for you and your children, the Child's Garden in a Can, put together by Clyde Robin Seed Company. The can comes complete with seed packets designed by children, a well-written instruction booklet that older children can read and follow, and string and stakes. Information on Clyde Robin Seed Company can be found at the end of Chapter 1.

Magic Beans

Try 'Royalty' or 'Royal Burgundy' bush or pole beans. These are tasty, deep purple string beans that are fun to grow. My children used to call them "magic beans" because after they have been in boiling water for two or three minutes, they turn green (much to the relief of people who can't imagine eating bright purple string beans). Where does the purple go?

Beans must be blanched before freezing, or the beans will be very soft when thawed. Blanching (boiling for a few minutes) destroys the enzyme that makes beans turn mushy. Purple beans are their own barometer to tell you how long to blanch them; when they turn green they are properly blanched.

Pole bean plants are great for making a bean tepee. (See the accompanying drawing for directions on how to make a bean tepee.) Particularly appropriate for bean tepees are scarlet and 'Dutch White' runner beans; they grow fast and very tall, and in some parts of the country they attract hummingbirds. (See Chapter 5 for instructions on how to save some of your bean seeds for next year.)

Colorful Corn

Corn is a good crop for children. The seeds are large enough for little fingers to handle and they sprout quickly. Corn generally has few pests, and it grows very fast. Picking and shucking the corn are enjoyable endeavors. Corn takes a lot of room and has some basic cultural requirements that limit where it can be planted. Before you can decide where to plant it, you must know that corn is wind-pollinated; therefore, it must be planted in blocks, not in a long, single row or in double rows. Corn planted in single or double rows usually produces few kernels. In addition, because of cross-pollination, sweet corn must be separated from popcorn and cornmeal varieties. Consequently, if you want more than one type, one type must be separated from another by a building, or different types must be planted one hundred feet or so apart. Different varieties of sweet corn do not need to be separated because it doesn't matter if they cross-pollinate. If you have only a small area for gardening, try one of the dwarf corn varieties. Even though the plants are small, most varieties have fairly good-size ears. Of course, you may want to see what happens if you plant corn in single rows; often we learn better by experiencing the reasons for rules. And there aren't many other areas of experience where children can deviate from given rules and not have serious consequences.

If you want a lesson in cross-pollination, plant a block of sweet yellow or white corn within ten or fifteen feet of a block of Hopi blue corn. What will happen? You will probably get ears of yellow (or white) corn with a few purple polka dots and purple corn with yellow (or white) dots. The purple kernels in the yellow ear will be a little tough, and the yellow kernels in the purple ear will not grind as easily. That's why gardeners are advised not to plant those corn varieties close together. Most people are not bothered by the cross-pollination.

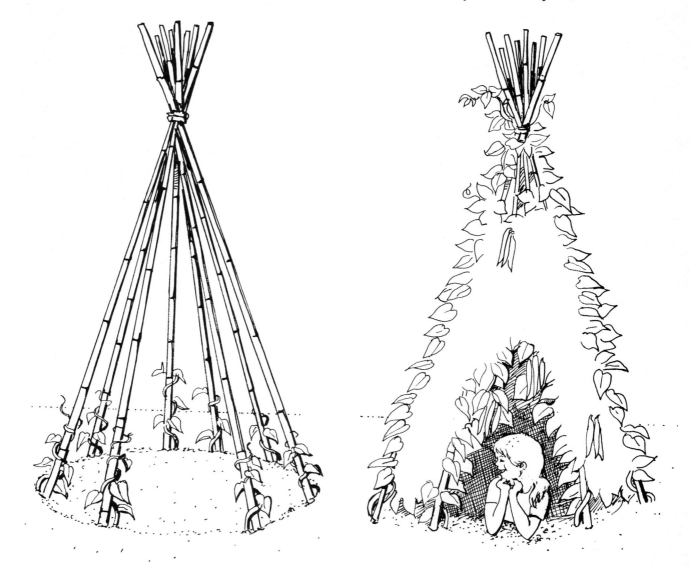

Regardless of what happens, the Hopi blue corn will make great cornmeal—blue corn is not usually eaten fresh on the cob. When the kernels are very dry, they will grind beautifully in the blender. Use the cornmeal to make some of the best cornbread and tamales you have ever tasted.

Grow popcorn, then pop it. There are all types of popcorn. Some varieties produce little yellow or white ears. 'Strawberry' popcorn produces miniature, rounded, reddish ears that look like large strawberries. For Christmas you can put strong wires in the ends and hang them on the tree or give them away as presents.

Dill, Fennel, and Butterfly Wings

Dill and fennel are closely related, fast-growing herbs. They should be planted in the spring and can be harvested throughout most of the summer. They grow easily, sometimes too easily, and often support the yellow-and-black-striped caterpillars of the swallowtail butterfly. In addition, because the nectar in the flowers is food for many other insects as well, the flowers become miniature entomology labs, often crawling with ladybugs, syrphid flies, and lacewings, all of which are predators of bothersome pests. The flowers are fragrant and useful in the kitchen, and they grow so readily that children can learn to share some of their garden with insects. Furthermore, dill and fennel are members of the same family, and the flowers, umbels, look the same. Knowing plant families is valuable for all gardeners. Related plants are carrots, caraway, anise, coriander, and celery.

Opposite Bean tepees are one of a child's favorite garden pleasures. Use wooden or bamboo poles to form a circle about four feet in diameter. Mulch the ground heavily with compost or other organic matter so that the soil will not get packed down. Outside the circle of poles plant vigorous varieties of pole beans, 'Sugar Snap' peas, or climbing peas such as scarlet runner beans.

Playhouse Bouquets

Children, like the rest of us, love flowers. Annuals such as marigolds, zinnias, cosmos, and pansies are easy to grow. Even easier for little ones to grow are bulbs such as crocus, hyacinths, and tulips. Make sure they don't put the bulbs in their mouths because some of them, such as daffodils and narcissus, are poisonous.

Gardening with flowers has infinite possibilities. Just being able to pick their own bouquets gives most children joy, not to mention taking daffodils to the teacher, arranging zinnias in a vase, drying statice and strawflowers for winter bouquets, making flower headbands, pressing wildflowers or johnny-jump-ups and mounting them to make greeting cards, making potpourris with fragrant roses, and decorating a Maypole with spring flowers. The pleasures of flowers seem endless.

Goobers—The Curious Nuts

There's something wondrous about peanuts. They flower, produce pegs from the flowers, and then the pegs burrow into the ground. A few months later when you pull up the plant, you will see clusters of peanuts hanging from the underground stems. Peanuts require a long, warm summer. If you live in a cooler area, choose Spanish peanuts because they can be grown farther north.

Potatoes—Nature's Treasure Hunt

If you plant potatoes in plenty of loose compost, you will have a large harvest and easy digging in the fall, even for little children. Harvesting potatoes is like going on a treasure hunt; it's one of my favorite gardening projects. Potatoes are started by cutting whole potatoes into pieces (each piece must have an eye) and planting each piece. If you try to grow potatoes purchased at the market, they usually rot in the ground before they sprout. Why? Because Americans don't like to see octopuslike white sprouts coming out of their potatoes; therefore, most potatoes have been sprayed with a growth-regulating hormone that inhibits sprouting.

One of the seed companies, Gurney's, carries blue potatoes, which are blue all the way through; all-yellow potatoes; and small, oblong, fingerling types. All are delicious and fun to grow.

Strawberries—Everybody's Favorite

Strawberries are rewarding for beginning gardeners because they are not too difficult to grow in most parts of the country. Combine some plants of a spring-bearing variety and plants of the ever-bearing type that will bear through part of the summer. If you have lim-

Peanuts are fun to grow. After they blossom, they send pegs down into the ground; the pegs develop into peanuts.

ited space, give your child his or her own strawberry jar. Strawberry plants can be put in all of the little pockets, or a combination of strawberries, violas, and alyssum can be planted.

Double Your Pleasure— Peppermint and Spearmint

Mint is easy to grow and pleasant to taste. Actually it is almost too easy to grow and can become a pest. Plant mint in a confined area. Dry some of the leaves by placing them in the oven, turned on to the lowest setting, and drink peppermint tea on a cold winter night. Have you ever noticed that mint has square stems?

Giant Jack-O'-Lanterns

Children love large pumpkins, so choose a large variety such as 'Big Max'. Plant the seeds as soon as frost is no longer a problem so there will be enough time to grow super-size pumpkins. In addition, your children can carve their initials on the fruits when they are just starting to form; then when the pumpkin is ripe, the initials will have grown and the jack-o'-lanterns will be personalized. Most jack-o'-lantern pumpkins don't make good pies, but the seeds are good when roasted.

Radishes—Red, White, and Black

Not all children like radishes, but if yours do, grow them because they are the fastest-growing edible. The seeds germinate quickly, and many varieties are ready to harvest in three to four weeks. There are many, many types of radishes: large, small, round, oblong, red, white; and some Oriental types are even black. Try the new radish called 'Easter Egg'; the radishes of this variety are different shades of red and pink.

Radishes grow best in the cool part of the year: spring and late summer. Use fertilizer and plenty of water so the plants will grow fast.

Squash and More Squash

If your child likes squash, zucchini is a good vegetable to grow. 'Burpee Hybrid' will produce nearly a zucchini a day, whether you want it or not. A golden variety, although not usually as prolific as the green, is sometimes better accepted by children. Chop up some of the flowers and float them in a bowl of soup. Spaghetti squash is interesting and delicious. When it's ripe, you can bake it, scrape out the strands of spaghettilike squash, and smother it in marinara or pesto sauce. Just writing this makes my mouth water.

Sunflower—King of the Garden

Sunflowers grow very big and tall, and young children get a charge out of being responsible for growing something so awesome. Sunflowers are a bonus for the birds. You and your children can present a sunflower head to the birds on Christmas morning.

Tomatoes and Their Horned Foes

Of all the types of tomatoes, cherry tomatoes grow the most easily and are just the right size for a child's mouth. 'Sweet 100' is a particularly tasty and prolific variety. Other varieties to try are one of the old-fashioned, large, fluted varieties; the small, yellow pear; or the striped 'Tigerella'. All of these will produce exclamations during "show and tell" at school. The seed companies mentioned at the end of Chapter 5 and at the end of this chapter are good sources for the seeds.

An interesting garden project involves the tomato hornworm, which is an extremely large caterpillar that thrives in most parts of the country and feeds on tomatoes. If you find a tomato hornworm on your plants, cut off the branch it's on (it will hold on for dear life), collect some foliage, and put the hornworm and the foliage in a large jar. (Hints on how to find a hornworm: Look for areas of the plant where whole leaves are missing. Then look for little piles of green geometric droppings; the caterpillar should be in the foliage above the droppings.)

Leave the hornworm in the jar while it eats its fill and pupates, probably a few days. Then remove the pupa from the jar and place it on top of the soil in a large flowerpot filled with potting soil. Watch it burrow down into the soil. Cover the pot with a plate and put the pot in a cool place for the winter. In late March or April bring in the pot, take off the plate, and

cover the pot with something that allows you to see what's going on, but that won't let the soon-to-emerge, large, spotted sphinx moth escape. Usually it will be a week or two before the moth emerges, and if you are exceedingly lucky, you may even see it come out and "pump up" its wings.

Sources of Information

Books

Brown, Marc. *Your First Garden Book*. Boston: Little, Brown and Company, 1981. A book of garden projects and delights for children.

Burnett, Frances Hodgson. *The Secret Garden*. New York: Lippincott, 1938. A classic story that I must have heard or read numbers of times. A wonderful, imaginative trip set in a garden.

Skelsey, Alice, and Huckaby, Gloria. *Growing Up Green*. New York: Workman Publishing, 1973.

Nurseries

Use the nurseries listed at the end of Chapter 5, particularly Johnny's Selected Seeds, Redwood City Seed Company, and Seeds Blum, to obtain varieties I have mentioned. Other companies that carry some of these varieties are listed below.

Gurney's Seed & Nursery Company
Yankton, SD 57079
Gurney's carries many vegetable seeds, including the purple beans and all kinds of seed potatoes.

Geo. W. Park Seed Company
P.O. Box 31
Greenwood, SC 29647
This company carries a wide range of vegetable and flower seeds.

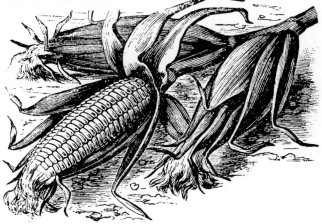

Chapter 11

The Moneysaving Garden

Who says money doesn't grow on trees? Homeowners expect their yards to cost them money. Few ever consider the possibility that instead of costing money, a yard actually can help save money. The average yard in this country consumes money in three major ways. First, hundreds of dollars are wasted because few yards are planned to take advantage of solar heating or basic cooling techniques for the house. Second, yards that have large lawns, particularly in the arid West, where constant watering is necessary, often have high maintenance costs. And, finally, few yards are designed to cut food and gift-giving expenses.

Heating and cooling experts estimate that up to 20 percent of air-conditioning bills and 20 to 30 percent of heating bills for residences can be cut by proper placement of the landscaping elements. The larger your yard, the more savings you can realize by strategically placing trees and shrubs. Well-placed evergreen shrubs and trees help cut down the effects of winter winds against the house; by removing evergreen shrubs and trees near the south-facing wall, the homeowner allows the winter sun to warm the wall. Conversely, in the summer, deciduous trees, shrubs, and vines can shade the south and west walls, preventing the heat from building up in the house. For more information on saving money through landscaping, see Ruth Foster's book, *Landscaping That Saves Energy Dollars*.

Lawn, the Great Money Sink

I've seen it happen time and time again. People who are on a tight budget think they cannot afford to spend a lot of money on the landscaping; so they go to the nursery, buy a package of grass seed, and turn most of their yard into a large lawn. There are few things you can do, particularly in the West, that will cost more over the long run. A lawn will nickel and dime you to death. Lawn mower, gas for the mower, lawn-mower maintenance, edger, water, sprinkler repairs, fertilizer, herbicides, fungicides, vacation maintenance: all for just a humdrum lawn. And a show-place lawn can cost you many hundreds of dollars a year. A well-maintained lawn needs to be aerated, thatched, reseeded, and top dressed every year. All of those expenses are just the tip of the iceberg. They don't even take into account that the lawn area could be covered with money-saving plants that would provide food for the table.

Lawn maintenance is big money in this country, and our whole system is set up to perpetuate it. If you have a lawn, use appropriate lawn maintenance techniques to save money and use fewer resources. Here are a few pointers.

1. Plan your lawn area to be as level as possible so that water and nutrients won't run off. Keep the lawn as small as possible. Don't plant lawn simply because you don't know what else to do.

2. Plan the area for ease of maintenance. Avoid spotting trees and shrubs in the lawn, and install mow strips (strips of concrete, brick, or wood that border a lawn and keep the wheels of the mower level at the edge, so when you mow, you also trim the edge), thereby cutting down on the amount of machine trimming. Furthermore, without trees the grass will grow thicker so that less weeding and fewer herbicides will be necessary.

3. No lawn grass species has low water or fertilizer needs, but some are a little better than others. Choose bluegrass and rye over bentgrass, which is a heavy feeder and needs lots of water. Breeders of grass seed are now aware of the problem and are hybridizing for grass varieties that use less water and fertilizer. Keep an eye out for new introductions.

4. Do not remove lawn clippings unless they are longer than an inch. Research has shown that turf is healthier and requires less fertilizer when the clippings are left in place. Grass clippings are equivalent to a 4-1-3 fertilizer, which means that two pounds of nitrogen per 1,000 square feet are saved on the average lawn. Contrary to popular opinion, thatch buildup is not a problem

5. Avoid so-called cheap fertilizer. It ain't! Nitrate fertilizers, in particular, are leached from the soil and volatilize into the air; plants get a quick fix of nitrogen, then soon need another shot. Except when the weather is cold, use organic manures or slow-release nitrogen fertilizers.

6. Mow the grass so it is 1-1/2 to 2 inches long. Most people cut the grass too short, causing it to thin out. Grass that is cut too short requires more water.

The Garden as Provider

Most homeowners realize that they can save money by growing some of their food, but few realize how much can be saved or how to make the greatest savings. A Gallup Poll conducted for *Gardens for All* (180 Flynn Avenue, Burlington, VT 05401) showed that in 1981 the average home gardener invested $25 in garden supplies and reaped $414 worth of produce. Those statistics related to an ordinary garden; an intensively grown vegetable garden can produce much more. Fruit trees and fruiting shrubs will provide additional food. An article in *The Family Food Garden* (November 1983) described a gardening family that grew $1,100 worth of crops for a family of seven on an acre in Minnesota. Dedicated gardeners obviously save a lot more money than those who want to be only somewhat involved.

Opposite Container gardening is possible even in an apartment or on a small patio. Three very productive varieties of vegetables that grow well in large containers are 'Gypsy' pepper, 'Gold Rush' zucchini, and 'Sweet 100' tomato.

Home-grown Gifts

A delightful way to save money is to plan your garden with gift giving in mind. At Christmas or for birthdays, homemade strawberry or kiwi jam, pickles, canned peaches, tomato juice, applesauce, dried fruit for a trail mix, and dried herbs are always a hit. So are dried-flower bouquets, so in the summer grow statice, strawflowers, yarrow, baby's breath, and many of the grasses with beautiful seed heads. Gifts from the yard are unusual and original.

If you occasionally buy flowers for the house, for a friend in the hospital, or if you enjoy taking a house gift when you go to a friend's house for a visit, consider growing your own cut flowers. If you are short on garden time, plant perennials and shrubs that are easy to grow and that produce flowers you can cut. Another idea for people who are short on time (aren't we all?) is to convert some of your lawn to a meadow and seed it heavily with wildflowers that are good for cutting. For winter giving consider growing and collecting some of the flowers and seed pods that dry well. Wreaths made of grapevines or wisteria can be dramatic when festooned with garlic heads and chilies for the kitchen, or with bittersweet and thistles for the front door.

Following is a list of flowers for cutting and for dried arrangements. Find out which ones will do well in your area.

The Home Florist

Have you priced flowers lately? Many exotic flowers are sold by the stem, which range in price from $2.50 to $5.00. You can add beauty to your home year after year by planting your flower garden today. The home florist always has a bouquet to give friends on birthdays and at other special times.

Perennials

Bird-of-paradise, black-eyed susan, chrysanthemum, coreopsis, forsythia, iris, lavender, lilac, lily, marguerite, old roses, Shasta daisy, and yarrow.

Annuals

Baby's-breath, bachelor's button, bells of Ireland, calendula, cosmos, marigold, nasturtium, nicotiana, pincushion flower, snapdragon, stock, sweet pea, and zinnia.

Bulbs

Anemone, daffodil, Dutch iris, freesia, narcissus, ranunculus, and tulips.

Flowers for Drying

Baby's-breath, bells of Ireland, Chinese lantern, globe amaranth, globe thistle, hydrangea, love-in-a-mist, money plant, safflower, statice, strawflower, yarrow, and many ornamental grasses.

Wildflowers

Black-eyed susan, California poppy (if seared), cattail, coreopsis, daisy, goldenrod, mullein, mustard, penstemon, prairie grasses, Queen Anne's lace, tiger lily, wild roses, and yarrow.

Kitchen Gifts

Dried herbs add zest to your cooking. You can change an ordinary salad, for example, into an interesting, tasty salad simply by adding some freshly dried herbs. A soothing cup of tea can be brewed from a mixture of several varieties of dried mint. Also, herbs, harvested from your garden and carefully dried, are an especially welcome gift.

Drying Herbs

Drying herbs is a simple, rewarding task. Dried herbs lose their potency with age, so you should renew your supply of them annually.

It is important when harvesting herbs—basil, borage, cilantro, marjoram, mint, parsley, oregano, rosemary, sage, and thyme—for drying that you pick those that have not yet flowered. Pick during the driest part of the day. If necessary, wash the plants quickly and pat them dry. On a piece of screening, carefully place the leaves in a single layer, with no overlapping. Leave the screens out in a warm room away from sunlight for five to seven days, stirring the leaves occasionally. If the air is very humid or if you must dry the herbs quickly, put them in a very low oven (140 degrees Fahrenheit) for a few hours, until they crumble fairly easily in your hand.

When the herbs are thoroughly dry, store them in airtight containers and put them in a cool, dark place. For gift-giving, put them in small jars and label them in a decorative manner.

Drying Flowers

Take a bouquet of home-grown, dried flowers to your hosts when you dine out or to a sick friend. Flowers are a personal, beautiful, inexpensive—when you grow your own—gift that is always appreciated. If you have no room in your garden for an individual cutting garden, interplant a few of the easy-to-grow, compact varieties in your perennial border or vegetable garden. Choose from globe amaranth, love-in-a-mist, safflower, statice, and strawflower: they are the easiest to grow and dry.

Harvest your flowers on a dry day just before they come into full bloom and bring them inside. Make small bunches of individual varieties and hang them in a warm, dry, fairly dark place—a dark corner of the kitchen or in the garage, perhaps. Once they are thoroughly dry, you can carefully arrange the flowers in baskets or vases and have them ready to give as gifts. Of course, you can enjoy them in your own home as well.

After you have become successful at drying the flowers mentioned above, try some of the following varieties: baby's-breath, bells of Ireland, celosia, Chinese lantern, goldenrod, grasses of all different types, heather, hollyhock, hydrangea, lavender, Queen Anne's lace, tansy, and yarrow.

Wreaths

Wreaths are cherished symbols and have been used by humans for eons. While they are usually associated with Christmas, wreaths of herbs, dried flowers, pine cones, and vines are enjoyed the year round. Useful as inexpensive house decorations and as gifts, wreaths from the garden are easily constructed.

A very simple wreath can be made of grapevines and other materials from the garden. Start with freshly pruned vines that are supple; dried-out vines will be hard to bend and weave. Determine the size of wreath you want to make: the thicker the vines, the larger the wreath should be because large vines are not as flexible as thin ones. If you want your wreath to be particularly symmetrical, start weaving it around a large bowl or round wastebasket. Because of the suppleness of the material and the ridges caused by the leaf stems, the woven vines tend to stay securely in place. When the wreath is the thickness you want, decorate it with clusters of dried flowers, herbs, grasses, and anything else that strikes your fancy.

$1.00

PRIZE MEDAL COLLECTION

COLUMBIAN PRIZE MEDAL AWARDED

| AWARDED GRAND PRIZE MEDAL AT THE WORLD'S FAIR | MOST ASTOUNDING OFFER EVER MADE
35 PACKAGES OF THE EARLIEST AND BEST VEGETABLE NOVELTIES.   POSTPAID FOR ONLY $1.00. | NOVELTY EXTRAS FREE WITH EVERY ORDER FOR THIS COLLECTION |

Asparagus—Standard variety.
Beet—Select Early Sort.
Beet—Buckbee's Improved Long Smooth Blood.
Beans—Buckbee's Rust Proof.
Cabbage—Standard Early.
Cabbage—Mammoth Late Bridgeport Drumh'd.
Carrot—Best Long Variety.
Cauliflower—Buckbee's Early Favorite.
Celery—Buckbee's Improved Golden Heart.
Corn—Sweet, Best Early Variety.
Corn—Salad.
NOTICE—The Prize Medal Collection is sold at the extra low price because made up before the busy season begins.   It cannot be broken.

Cress—Fine Curled or Pepper Grass.
Cucumber—Fine Table Variety.
Cucumber—Early Cluster.
Lettuce—Best Head or Cabbage Variety.
Melon—Musk, True Osage.
Melon—Musk. Select Early Sort.
Melon—Water, New Dixie.
Melon—Water, Fine Variety.
Onion—Buckbee's Danvers.
Onion—Fine Pickling Variety.
Parsnip—Long Sugar.
Parsley—Curled.
Peas—Earliest Variety.
Pepper—Mountain Sweet.

Radish—Best Turnip Variety.
Radish—Lady Finger.
Sage.
Spinach—New Round Leaf.
Squash—Select Winter Variety.
Squash—New Crookneck.
Turnip—Buckbee's Purple Top.
Turnip—Ruta Baga.
Tomato—Fine Red Variety.
Tomato—Best Fancy Sort.

10 Choice Flowering Bulbs Free with Every Order for the Prize Medal Collection.

While the price of seeds *has* gone up since the issue of this ad in a 1909 seed catalog, $15 worth of seeds can still produce hundreds of dollars worth of vegetables.

Opposite, top Shown here, early in the season, is a portion of Vicki Sebastiani's Italian vegetable garden. In the foreground are tomato plants on wire cages; farther back are melons; and in the raised beds are eggplants, onions, and young summer vegetables.

Bottom Succulent young vegetables from the gourmet grocery store are a treat few people can afford. From the author's garden, left to right, are 'Tiny Tim' cherry tomatoes; 'Gold Rush' zucchini; baby romaine lettuces; red, white, and yellow young beets; young wax beans; half-developed lemon cucumbers; and very young carrots.

Page 166, top The Fancys' backyard has been transformed from a basketball court to an edible landscape with raised beds. Ninety percent of the plants in the photograph are edible. Included are a number of dwarf citrus and fruit trees and numerous annual edibles, such as tomatoes, eggplants, summer squash, peppers, herbs, and strawberries. Flowers are added for color and for cutting. A true pleasure garden, it produces bounty as well as beauty. (Landscape design: Rosalind Creasy)

Bottom Fresh produce from the Fancys' garden enriches the quality and variety of food on the table.

Page 167, clockwise from left Nowhere is it written: Thou shalt not grow flowers with your vegetables.

A grapevine trained on a south-facing wall can perform the herculean task of saving money for you, and its lush green foliage is beautiful. In summer the leaves shade the house, thereby reducing air-conditioning expenses. In fall it produces grapes, to be eaten fresh or dried as raisins. In winter it loses its leaves, letting in the sun to warm the house, and in spring the prunings can be saved to make grapevine wreaths for gift-giving all through the year.

Grow your own ginger as a gourmet treat. Young green ginger shoots can be added to stir-fried dishes; and as a bonus, it is a lush green container plant.

Page 168, clockwise from top left Kate Gessert is harvesting salad makings from her cottage pleasure garden. Among the wonderful additions to her salad are homemade herb vinegars and edible nasturtium and chive flowers.

Children particularly enjoy picking flowers and strawberries from the garden.

Kate Gessert's frontyard flower/vegetable border delights passersby. The decorative kales and chrysanthemums are the real stars in early fall.

Even the smallest corner can produce a pleasure garden. Here bronze fennel provides leaves and flowers for a salad and also attracts butterflies. In the barrel are geraniums and violas; both have edible flowers.

Edible Gardens—Moneysavers

Time is one of the factors that determine how much money you can save by gardening. How much time do you have to garden and how much time do you have for harvesting and preserving food? For a vegetable garden, planting time is needed in the spring and quite a bit of time is needed for harvesting in late summer. For the garden I recommend, plan to devote a few days in the spring to prepare the soil and to start annual vegetables. If your space is limited and you are going to put in French intensive beds, you will need twenty or thirty additional hours the first year to install the beds. After your soil is prepared and the seedlings are in, you will need three or four hours a week throughout the summer to weed, to tie up vines, to put in transplants, to harvest, and perhaps to water.

Not only is time necessary, but so is timing: putting in the time when it is needed. If you are a teacher, say, you may have plenty of time in the summer but little when school starts. For you, picking beans through the summer or making delicacies from edibles that produce in spring or summer, such as pickled beets and strawberry jam, may be no problem. However, your dreams of canning spaghetti sauce and making salsa from your dozen tomato plants that ripen in September, when new students need attention, would be disappointing and frustrating.

Another factor to consider is garden space. Some people create a problem here where none exists; or, at least, if there is a problem, it is usually easily solved. Many folks tell me that they would like to have a vegetable garden, but they don't have the space. People seem to confuse having space with owning the garden. My partner and I gardened for years in a neighbor's unused dog run. Garden space abounds in this country. Many cities and towns have community gardens; if yours doesn't, you

probably know a neighborly senior citizen or a friend who would be delighted to share space in return for some of your harvest. It doesn't take much room to produce a lot of food.

A final important factor is your selection of edibles. Dwarf fruit trees give more yield for the space than full-size trees. Pole beans yield more beans than bush types. Vining cucumbers and melons yield more produce than bush types. Choose from the following list of high-yielding vegetables and fruits those that grow well in your area.

Vegetables

Artichokes, asparagus, basil, beans, beets, chard, cucumbers, eggplants, garlic, leeks, lettuce, parsley, peppers, scallions, shallots, snow peas, sorrel, sprouts, tomatoes, and zucchini.

Fruits

Alpine strawberries, apples, apricots, avocados, blackberries, blueberries, cherries, chestnuts, grapefruits, kiwis, lemons, mangoes, oranges, papayas, peaches, pears, pecans, pineapples, plums, raspberries, rhubarb, and strawberries.

Here are some other suggestions for planning your moneysaving food garden.

1. Interplant quick-growing annuals such as radishes and lettuce among your slow-growing vegetables.

2. Plant seeds when possible. Vegetable plants from the nursery are expensive. Save your own seeds from year to year when possible. (See Chapter 5 for information on saving seeds.)

3. If your space is limited, plant in intensively prepared beds. (Read *How to Grow More Vegetables* by John Jeavons for instructions on bed preparation.)

4. Compost anything you can get your hands on. Some city park departments distribute

leaves and clippings to homeowners who want them for mulch and compost.

5. Use dwarf fruit trees whenever possible to produce more fruit from a limited area. The trees are dwarf, but the fruit is full size.

6. Replace barren ornamental plants with edibles. Many of the standard fruit trees and shrubs have long been overlooked as landscape material. Beautiful edibles such as blueberries, apples, almonds, plums, persimmons, and cherries, just to mention a few, have been overlooked in favor of flowering crabs, dogwoods, and forsythia.

7. If space is at a premium, avoid space-wasting plants such as winter squash, pumpkins, and corn.

8. Plant gourmet vegetables to help cut down on your entertaining costs.

Another way to save money is to preserve some of your harvest for winter eating, when produce prices are up. The most economical way to preserve some vegetables and fruits, such as carrots, potatoes, beets, cabbage, turnips, apples, and pears, is to put them in a root cellar; although drying is economical for apricots, peaches, plums, grapes, tomatoes, and herbs.

A Moneysaving Backyard

The accompanying diagram shows a very small backyard full of bountiful, yet beautiful, plants: they do double duty. There are genetic dwarf fruit trees: two apples, a peach, and a pear. These flowering and fruiting large shrubs make quite a delightful background for the patio area. On either side are black and red raspberry bushes trained on decorative trellises and clusters of blueberry bushes. On both sides of the patio and in the middle of the back planting bed is a combination vegetable and flower border, which is planted with extra-productive species such as tomatoes, snow peas, chard, peppers, and eggplants and flowers that are good for cutting, such as calendulas, statice, coreopsis, and baby's-breath.

The patio has containers for vegetables and herbs and is covered with an arbor that has two kiwi vines on it. Grapevines are espaliered on the south wall on either side of the house; with the kiwi vines on the arbor they provide shade on hot days and help cut air-conditioning bills. In addition, the grape prunings can be used to make wreaths in the winter.

Raspberries can be one of the biggest moneysavers in your garden.

Opposite A moneysaving garden can be as small as this patio garden, which includes many features: it shades the house in summer, it provides flowers for gift-giving, and it produces vegetables and fruits for the table.
1. Genetic dwarf peach, 'Honey Babe'
2. Genetic dwarf apple, 'Garden Delicious'
3. Black raspberries
4. Herb jar
5. Strawberries
6. Blueberries, three different varieties
7. Kiwi vine, female
8. Rhubarb
9. Grapevine trained on wall
10. Genetic dwarf pear, 'Golden Prolific'
11. Red raspberries
12. Peppers in container
13. Zucchini in container
14. Cherry tomato in container
15. Kiwi vine, male

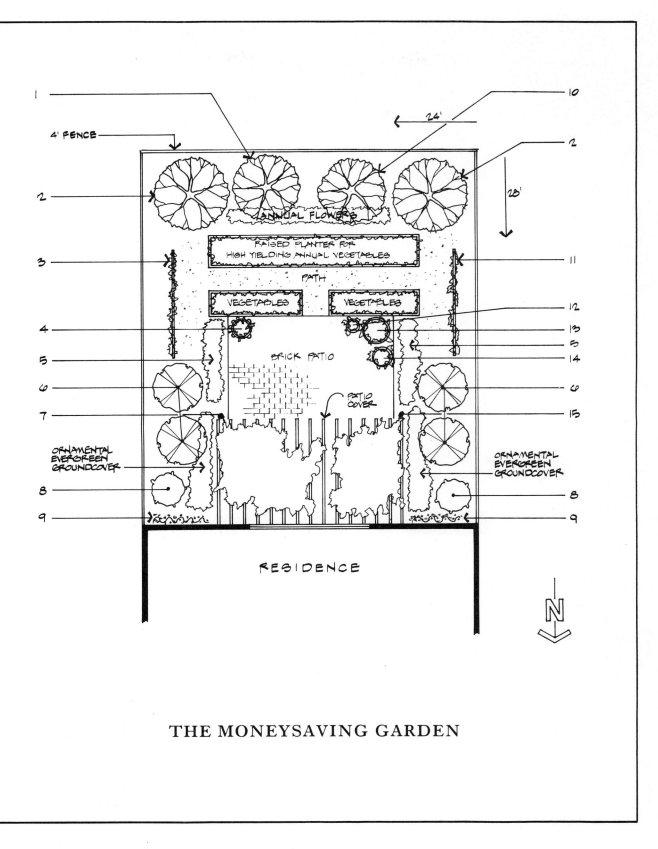

THE MONEYSAVING GARDEN

Recycled Materials

The materials are usually the most expensive items in any garden construction project. Projects using brick, stone, and concrete can make the budget groan. One way around the high cost of some of these items is to use recycled materials.

With the detailed plans in front of you, figure the dimensions of the items you want to construct. Then look at the list that follows and consider which recycled materials you may be able to use. If you must make adjustments, it will be simpler to make them on paper than after you have begun construction. For instance, railroad ties generally come in eight-foot lengths. They are hard to cut; therefore, if you are using them for a planter, it would make sense to design the planter with eight-foot increments in mind.

Recycled materials are available from a number of different sources, and one source may even be your own yard. I recycled the grapestakes from my own fence after the posts and stringers had rotted away. I reused bricks from my old patio that was buckled by some very invasive tree roots. I didn't have enough bricks to make the new patio as large as I wanted, so I purchased 400 new ones, then made a pattern that combined the old and the new bricks. (You can see my recycled backyard, with its brick patio, grapestake fence, and railroad-tie planter on page iv.) Other sources of recycled materials are contractors, demolition yards, nursery supply houses, and friends and neighbors.

1. Concrete. Recycled concrete, broken into 12-inch to 24-inch pieces, can be used as paving material for patios, paths, utility areas, retaining walls, and steps. You can recycle concrete from your own yard or from a nearby demolition project. If you decide to have the contractor dump a load of broken concrete in your front yard, you will have a disposal problem; that is, what to do with the pieces that are stained or too large or too small to use in your project. To avoid that problem it may be better to pick up the pieces at the demolition site. Concrete is very heavy, and only a limited number of pounds can be carried at one time in the average car. Therefore, it behooves you to locate the concrete as close as possible to your yard. You will find concrete of different shades of gray and beige and made with different types of aggregates. Try to choose batches of compatible colors when combining concrete from more than one source. For paths, pieces of broken concrete can be set in sand and mortared in place or left unmortared and planted between the cracks with herbs or low groundcovers. For walls less than two feet high, the pieces can be mortared, or the areas between the slabs can be filled with soil and planted with cascading types of flowers and herbs. Walls over two feet high, of any type of material, including recycled concrete, should be built by a licensed contractor and overseen by a structural engineer.

2. Old lumber can be gathered from demolition sites, old barns, and sometimes from the beach. Used telephone poles and railroad ties are usually available from nursery supply houses. Pieces of new wood, usable but often in short lengths, are sometimes available from construction sites. Usually it is wood suitable for inside construction, which must be painted or treated with wood preservative if you are going to use it outside.

Old railroad ties are probably the most versatile recycled construction material of all. They can be placed horizontally for steps, planters, short walls, and decking; they can be placed vertically for retaining walls. Their major drawback is their price. Railroad ties have been treated with creosote, which, while protecting the wood from the elements, can sometimes ooze out and get on clothing or stain carpeting when it is tracked inside on shoes.

Sources of Information

Books

Contact your local university extension office for brochures and booklets on how to grow fruits and vegetables in your area and how to preserve them.

Foster, Ruth. *Landscaping That Saves Energy Dollars.* New York: David McKay Co., 1978. A detailed text covering the many ways that landscaping can help cut energy bills.

Jeavons, John. *How to Grow More Vegetables.* Palo Alto, Calif.: Ecology Action of the Midpeninsula, 1974. A primer on French intensive gardening.

Schuler, Stanley, and Schuler, Elizabeth Meriwether. *Preserving the Fruits of the Earth.* New York: Dial Press, 1973. A book that is hard to find but worth looking for. It covers in detail how to preserve nearly everything.

Nurseries

Pine Tree Seed Company
P.O. Box 1399
Portland, ME 04104
Pine Tree is an unusual vegetable seed company because it sells inexpensive packages of vegetable seeds that contain only a few seeds of each variety—after all, how many of us use fifty tomato seeds?

Consumer Note

Sometimes homeowners get carried away and buy unnecessary equipment. Avoid, as much as possible, buying rarely used yard tools and gadgets. Consider renting a large tiller rather than buying one—it's probably cheaper in the long run. In addition, when you do buy tools, buy good ones. A fine fork and shovel made of forged steel with hardwood handles can last a lifetime; cheaply made tools often last only one season.

Smith & Hawken Tool Company
25 Corte Madera Avenue
Mill Valley, CA 94941
This company is known for its vast collection of superior garden tools.

Chapter 12
The Cottage Garden

The early Puritans left their mark on us in a number of subtle ways, some of which make life a series of joyless tasks. Sometimes I think their devotees must write garden books. The tone of many of the how-to books reeks of rules, admonitions, and dicta. How about a garden that is programmed to give you joy, to take care of you. Previous chapters of this book have given you ways to cut down on many of the usual garden chores, thus leaving you more time to spend in a meaningful way. This chapter is designed to give you the means to glory in the new-found time. The cottage garden is an outright celebration of what a garden can do for every part of you: colors to see, textures to touch, fragrances to smell, bird calls to hear, and myriad tastes for the palate. And, of course, we can't forget the most important part, your soul. You will experience the renewal of life, that primordial urge to believe in the future. You will put your fingers on the emerging carrot seedlings, anticipate the taste of the first tomato, and feel delight when the hummingbird visits the sage and the monarch butterfly sips from the dew collected by the nasturtium leaf.

I am suggesting that you plant a rather hedonistic variation of the traditional mixed border. Put it where you usually see a conventional shrub or flower border—along a fence line, for instance, or along a walk or driveway, next to the patio, or along shallow hillsides. Fill it with joy, with colors, tastes, fragrances, and even tactile pleasures—a swath of flowers and foliage.

The mixed border, sometimes called the perennial border since it usually includes a large number of perennially blooming plants, has been in fashion since the late nineteenth century. It has its roots in the English cottage garden, and, at its best, the border is a subtle work of form, texture, and color—all used together to delight the soul. Properly planned, the border changes with the seasons.

Traditionally the staples in the mixed border were nonedible flowers, mostly perennials, with a sprinkling of annuals for quick color. Popular perennial flower choices for this type of ornamental border were iris, peony, phlox, dahlia, daisy, chrysanthemum, poppy, and the like. A new variation in today's perennial border is the addition of beautiful edibles such as ruby chard and flowering kale; plus a number of savory and attractive herbs such as variegated sage and dill; edible flowers such as nasturtium and carnation for your salads and desserts; and, to add still another dimension, fragrance, choose sweet-smelling lavender and stock. For many more choices, see the lists of flowers and beautiful edibles later in this chapter.

Think of the pleasure these gardens can give. Imagine having your barbecue on the back patio surrounded by bright borders of nasturtiums, violas, geraniums, and many herbs and edibles. You could reach over and pick a few leaves of spicy basil to put on your guest's still-warm tomato slices. Then you could harvest some of the nasturtium and viola flowers to add zip to your salad. Throughout the meal the fragrance of alpine strawberries would hint of the dessert to come, and the light fragrance of peppermint geraniums and lavender would perfume the air.

Your cottage garden could be near the front walk to welcome guests with fragrance and color. Or if your space is limited, you could even plant your pleasure border in the strip between the street and the sidewalk the way the Gessert family did in Oregon. (See page 178 for a detailed description of their garden.)

In planning your pleasure border, keep in mind these simple guidelines.

1. Make the border less than three feet wide, or provide a path or access on both sides of the beds so you'll be able to pick flowers and edibles and perform maintenance tasks.

2. Choose plants that require the same soil, water, and exposure.

3. If you are covering a large area, your design could depend on large quantities of one or two types of plants to unify the border, to create a theme to pull the border together for the eye.

4. There are two ways to work with color in these flower borders: (1) you can limit yourself to three or four basic colors, with one of them serving as an accent (for example, use red, orange, and yellow with an accent, a dash of blue); or (2) work with variations on one color theme (combining blues, lavenders, and pinks, for instance). Or throw caution to the wind, put in your favorite plants, and see what happens. Some people think that all flowers go well together, others don't; it seems to be a matter of personal taste. While it addresses itself to only a few edibles and herbs, a good resource on color design with plants is *Gardening with Color—Ideas for Planning and Planting with Annuals, Perennials, and Bulbs* by Margaret Brandstrom Pavel.

5. Think about the height your plants will be when they are full-grown. Consider height as a distinct design element; thus, tall plants will be at the back of the border while shorter ones will be toward the front.

6. Try to choose as many "double-duty" plants as you can; that is, choose those that have both colorful flowers as well as edible or fragrant flowers.

7. Choose attractive varieties of edibles for your border. Some vegetables and some varieties of vegetables are not particularly suited to a mixed border. For example, large vining squashes and pumpkins usually climb all over their neighbors; brussels sprouts usually get top-heavy and rangy with age; potatoes need to die back and turn yellow before they can be harvested. (See the list of suitable edibles later in this chapter.)

Caution: Because, for the most part, you are using edible plants and flowers to fill these borders, exclude ornamental plants that are poisonous. Poisonous flowers you might be tempted to use but should avoid are sweet peas, autumn crocus, bleeding-heart, foxglove, lantana, and larkspur. Also, don't interplant the edibles with ornamentals that need to be sprayed with pesticides.

Planning and Preparation

"Choose a sunny area where you would like to see your pleasure garden. Then envision the area as a three-dimensional painting or a colored sculpture—with lots of textures, colors, and shapes. Only what *you* are creating grows! The fact that you are creating a work of living art adds a whole dimension of chance and excitement to the creation." So says Kate Gessert, an experienced pleasure gardener and author of the book *The Beautiful Food Garden.* Unlike many food gardeners, she has been interested not only in how vegetables and fruits grow and taste, but also in how those edibles look in the garden. In fact, she was so interested that she managed a test plot of over one thousand varieties of annual vegetables at Oregon State University. As overseer, she evaluated the ornamental aspects and tastiness of the plants and included much of the information in her book. In an effort to share her experience and her vision of a pleasure garden, she has put together the following comments and recommendations.

"When you put in your pleasure garden, first, make sure that you have chosen a sunny, well-drained site. Next, incorporate plenty of organic matter; healthy plants are beautiful and productive plants.

"I love the way gardens are when various kinds of plants are all mixed up together. I enjoy working in these gardens, being in the middle of them, looking out into a forest of deeply cut zucchini leaves, big round seed heads of leek, graceful, sweetly scented lily flowers, and rampant caged tomatoes.

"I also enjoy the planning process, dreaming in winter and spring about what we'll grow the

The Gesserts enjoy the continual changes in their sidewalk flower/vegetable border. (If your sidewalk garden has heavy automobile traffic nearby, rinse your vegetables in a 5-percent vinegar solution to remove the lead that may be deposited on them.)

next season. In particular, I enjoy planning the flower-vegetable-herb bed that we plant in front of our house in the planting strip between the sidewalk and the street.

"In spring, after working in plenty of organic matter, I sowed kale, leeks, and parsnips. Later, I added rhubarb chard, celery, and chrysanthemums, with short-term fillers—coriander, lettuce, and California poppies. These were replaced in late summer by carrots and ornamental kale, which really came into full color after the first frost. That fall the rhubarb-chard leaves turned a deep mahogany, and nearby were the yellow and red chrysanthemums and the bright green foliage of parsnips and carrots. In another part of the bed I used cooler colors: grayish foliages and pink and purple flowers. With the purple-leaved 'Coral Queen' flowering kale, I planted 'Fragrance' carnation, burnet (a cucumber-flavored herb with a rosette of delicate blue green foliage), fall 'Violet Carpet' aster, 'Dwarf Blue Scotch' curly kale, leeks, artichokes, and wine red and lavender chrysanthemums. The combination was spectacular!

"Now it's late fall, and we're mulching the borders and planting spring bulbs. Already we are planning next year's pleasure; we will enjoy snowdrops near the burnet, ornamental alliums near the leeks, and iris reticulata near the ruby chard."

Look at the accompanying plans and pictures of the bed Kate designed. In particular, notice the arrangement of the different plants. The vegetables such as leeks and carrots, which you usually associate with long, straight rows, are clumped together instead. Nowhere is it written that vegetables have to grow in straight rows. In fact, that is not usually the most productive configuration. Straight rows have met the cultural needs of agriculture and its equipment, but the home gardener can produce more food per square foot by using wide rows or clumps. As Kate says, "Ornamental plants seldom look their best in long, straight rows—picture tulips or daffodils planted that way. Vegetables look best in clusters and arranged in pleasing shapes."

Choose your pleasure plants from the list that follows. On the list there are plants that give fragrance, taste, and a bounty of color and texture. Some of the flowers are edible and are delightful in salads or floating on a clear soup; many of the flowers are suitable for cutting and drying. Think how nice it will be to save money on flower buying, as well as to give bouquets

that don't have a "canned" appearance, as so many purchased ones do. And they're always the same varieties of flowers. Your bouquets will have an individual touch that reflects you, not the florist. Check to make sure that the flowers and vegetables you choose grow well in your area.

Opposite To get the most out of your cottage border, plan for as long a season as possible. As you can see here, the Gesserts make substitutions for spent plants and think ahead to the next season, taking advantage of every square inch of garden area.

1. Alyssum
2. Asparagus, interplanted with kochia in the summer
3. Coreopsis, 'Brown Eyes'
4. Dahlia, 'Terpo'
5. Artichoke, 'Green Globe'
6. Chrysanthemum, lavender and burgundy red, interplanted with 'Barrett Browning' narcissus in the fall
7. Anemone, 'Max Vogel'
8. Dahlia, pink
9. Clarkia in the spring; *Zinnia linearis* in the summer
10. Helenium, 'Butterpat'; interplanted with 'Carbineer' narcissus in the fall
11. Swiss chard, 'Rhubarb'
12. Chrysanthemum, 'Freedom'
13. Parsnip, 'Hollow Crown Improved'
14. Bunching onion, 'Japanese'
15. Kale, 'Dwarf Blue Curled Vates'
16. Leek, 'Unique'
17. Celery, 'French Dinant'
18. Chrysanthemum, 'Fireside'
19. Lettuce, 'Red Salad Bowl' in the spring; 'Portola Giant' gaillardia in the summer
20. Sage, 'Joseph'
21. Sage, 'Broadleaf'
22. Viscaria, 'Maggie May', in the spring; 'Coral Queen' flowering kale in the late summer
23. Aster, 'Violet Carpet'; interplanted with snowdrops in the fall
24. Petunia throughout the summer; interplanted with 'Minnow' narcissus in the fall
25. Coriander in the spring and summer; 'Early Red Ball' beets in the late summer
26. California poppy, 'Sundew'; 'Royal Chantenay' carrots in the late summer
27. Thyme, 'Dwarf Compact'
28. Carnation, 'Fragrance', interplanted with *Iris reticulata* in the fall
29. Burnet
30. Thyme, creeping

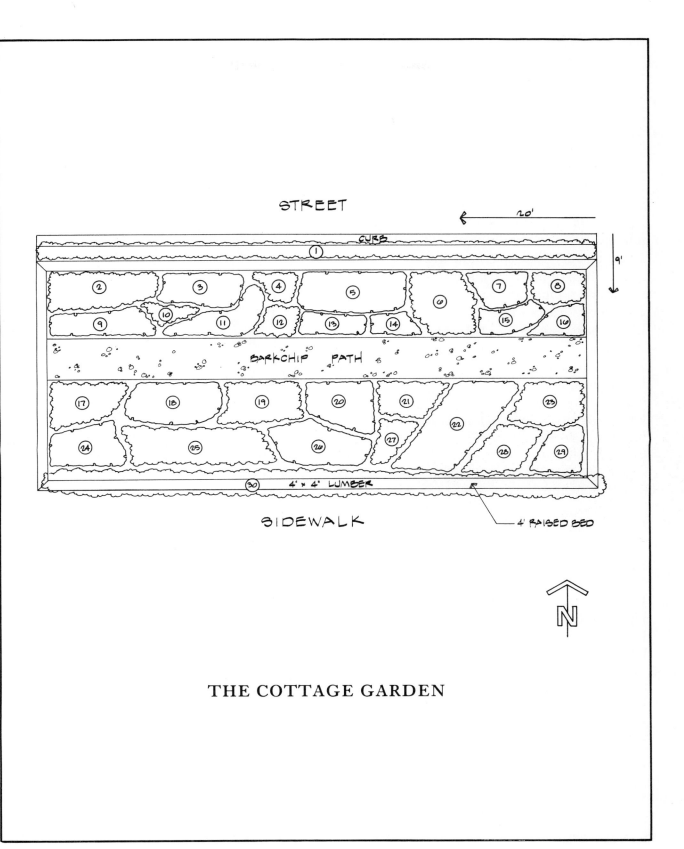

THE COTTAGE GARDEN

Edible Flowers

Borage, *Borago officinalis*
Calendula, *Calendula officinalis*
Carnation, *Dianthus Caryophyllis* species
Chamomile, *Matricaria recutita*
Chrysanthemum, *Chrysanthemum morifolium*
Cottage pink, *Dianthus plumarius*
Daylily, *Hemerocallis* species
Dill, *Anethum graveolens*
Fennel, *Foeniculum vulgare*
Garlic chives, *Allium tuberosum*
Geranium (scented), *Pelargonium* species
Gladiolus, *Gladiolus* species
Hollyhock, *Alcea rosea*
Johnny-jump-up, *Viola tricolor*
Lavender, *Lavandula officinalis*
Nasturtium, *Tropaeolum majus*
Peony, *Paeonia* species
Petunia, *Petunia hybrida*
Poppy, *Papaver* species (not opium)
Primrose, *Primula vulgaris*
Rose, *Rosa* species
Safflower, *Carthamus tinctorius*
Squash blossoms, *Cucurbita* species
Tulip, *Tulipa* species
Viola, *Viola cornuta*

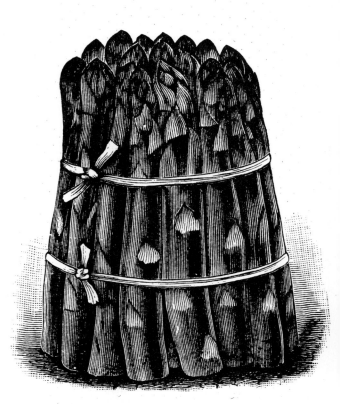

Recommended Varieties of Edibles

Artichoke, 'Globe'
Asparagus, 'Mary Washington'
Basil, 'Dark Opal', Sweet
Beans (bush), 'Royal Burgundy', 'Tender Crop', 'Rhemus'
Cabbage, 'Red Danish', 'Red Savoy', 'Stonehead', 'Ice Queen'
Celery, 'Summer Pascal', 'Burpee's Fordhook'
Chard (Swiss), 'Rhubarb'
Chrysanthemum greens, Shungiku types
Eggplant, 'Midnight', 'Japanese Purple Pickling', 'Black Beauty'
Endive, 'Green-Curled Ruffec'
Kale, 'Green-Curled Scotch', ornamental types

Lettuce, 'Dark Green Cos', 'Oakleaf', 'Red Salad Bowl', 'Salad Bowl'

Mustard, 'Fordhook Fancy', 'Prizewinner Curled Long'

Okra, red

Parsley, 'Champion Moss Curled', 'Dark Green Italian', 'Deep Green'

Peanuts, most varieties

Peas, 'Novella'

Peas (edible pods), 'Sugar Ann', 'Dwarf Gray Sugar'

Peppers, 'Red Chili', 'Hot Hungarian Yellow Wax', 'Golden Bell', 'Gypsy'

Strawberries, most varieties, particularly Alpine

Tomatoes, 'Floramerica', 'Roma', 'Red Cherry', 'Salad Master'

Zucchini, 'Gold Rush', 'Delicata', 'Bush Table Queen'

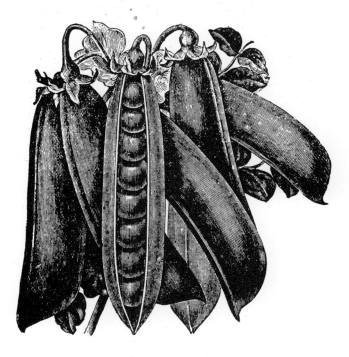

Herbs for a Decorative Border

Borage, burnet, chamomile, chives, dill, fennel, perilla, saffron crocus, and sage.

Flowers for a Decorative Border

The following list contains flowers that combine well with the edibles listed above; the starred flowers include varieties that are particularly good for cutting.

anemone*
baby's-breath*
bachelor's-button*
coreopsis*
cosmos*
forget-me-not
lobelia
marigold*
nicotiana
penstemon*
pincushion flower*
rudbeckia*

salvia*
santolina
snapdragon*
statice*
strawflower*
stock*
sweet William*
tansy
tithonia*
yarrow*
zinnia*

Sources of Information

Books

Creasy, Rosalind R. *The Complete Book of Edible Landscaping*. San Francisco: Sierra Club Books, 1982. How to use edible plants for beauty in the garden. It covers fruits and vegetables for the whole country.

Diamond, Denise. *Living with the Flowers*. New York: Quill, 1982. This book literally brings flowers into your life. It covers the subjects of edible flowers, how to dry flowers, gardening with flowers, even flower fairies.

Gessert, Kate Rogers. *The Beautiful Food Garden*. New York: Van Nostrand Reinhold Co., 1983. Gessert's book covers in great detail how to landscape with edibles and combine flowers and vegetables, as well as selections of the most beautiful vegetables and herbs.

Midda, Sara. *In and Out of the Garden*. New York: Workman Publishing, 1981. A poetic, visual delight for those who love living things.

Pavel, Margaret Brandstrom. *Gardening with Color—Ideas for Planning and Planting with Annuals, Perennials, and Bulbs*. San Francisco: Ortho Books, 1977. This book describes how to use flowering plants in the garden.

White, Katherine S. *Onward and Upward in the Garden*. New York: Farrar, Straus & Giroux, 1979. One woman's delightful view of gardening.

Nurseries

The following nurseries have excellent selections of ornamental annual vegetables and edible flowers.

Nichols Herb and Rare Seeds
1190 North Pacific Highway
Albany, OR 97321

Geo. W. Park Seed Company
P.O. Box 31
Greenwood, SC 29646

Redwood City Seed Company
P.O. Box 361
Redwood City, CA 94064
Catalog 50 cents.

Seeds Blum
Idaho City Stage
Boise, ID 83707
Catalog $1.

Acknowledgments

No one person has the range of garden experience and technical expertise represented in this book. I needed help from many different people. Numerous authorities in many specialized horticultural fields shared their knowledge. A host of plant people—passionate gardeners—generously shared their gardens and vast experience. And, of course, there was the guidance of numerous book people—people whose passion it is to produce a beautiful and meaningful book.

Let me start with my friends and cohorts whose involvement with this book was global. Marcie Hawthorne, whose love of life is brought to the world through her pen, not only illustrated this book but also was directly involved with many other aspects. When I needed photos of Italian vegetables, she grew the vegetables. When I needed information on chaparral gardening or when I needed to locate other gardeners, she helped. In addition, and of most importance, Marcie was my soulmate, lending her support and inspiration whenever it was needed. Another valuable source of support and information came from Kit Anderson of Gardens For All in Vermont. Her hospitality made my northeastern research a joy, and often I have called her for information and resources. Kate Gessert of Oregon generously shared her gardening expertise and contacts, located photos and gardens, and gave me a base of operations while I learned about northwestern gardens. Suzanne Lipsett is editor par excellence; her organizational and editing help was invaluable. Robert Creasy generously tutored me in the ways of the computer and helped me hone my photographic skills; and his high standards are evident throughout the book. Jane McKendall, my business partner and dear friend, kept things running smoothly and provided an always-available ear to help me think things through. Daniel Hawthorne gave enthusiastic support, and his meticulous construction of my garden gave me the perfect environment for my research. Karla Patterson, director of education at the Morton Arboretum, made my study of the prairie as rewarding and inspirational as possible, and Peg Creasy was my guide and noble assistant on tours of the East Coast. I thank them.

Throughout my years of research many experts in horticultural and environmental fields were generous with their help. They were: Pat Armstrong, Morton Arboretum, an expert on prairie restoration; Russell Beatty, landscape architect, University of California at Berkeley; Faith Thompson Campbell, Natural Resources Defense Council; Craig Tufts, National Wildlife Fund; Ruth Troetschler, biologist and bird enthusiast; Roger Del Moral, professor of environmental botany, University of Washington. Native plant authorities who assisted me were Barry Coate, horticultural consultant; Art Kruckeberg, professor of botany, University of Washington; and Cliff Schmidt, professor of botany, San Jose State University. Wildflower experts who assisted me were Steve Atwood, Clyde Robin Seed Company; the staff of Vermont Wildflower Farm; and Judith Lawry, Larner Seeds. Heirloom vegetable experts were Jan Blum and Karla Prabucki, Seeds Blum; Carolyn Jabs, writer and expert on heirloom seeds; and John Withee, heirloom bean expert. Rose authorities were Beverly R. Dobson and Pat Wiley, owner of Roses of Yesterday and Today. Authorities on orchids include Steve Hawkins and Marvel Sherril of McLellan's Acres of Orchids, Rebecca Tyson Northern, Randy Peterson, and Sue Johnson.

In addition I received help in locating information and gardeners from John Dotter, administrator of Prusch Park, San Jose, California; Robert Kourik, edible landscaper, Sonoma, California; Steve Frowine, Burpee Seeds, Warminster, Pennsylvania; the staff of Gardens For All, Burlington, Vermont; Grigsby's Cactus Gardens, Vista, California; Geo. W. Park Seeds, Greenwood, South Carolina; *Organic Gardening and Farming* magazine staff, Emmaus, Pennsylvania; and Jamie Jobb of The Howe Homestead of Walnut Creek, California. The staff of a number of arboretums were extremely helpful, including Longwood Gardens, Kennet Square, Pennsylvania; Missouri Botanical Garden, St. Louis, Missouri; and the Morton Arboretum, Lisle, Illinois.

Besides the gardens described in this book, the following people shared their gardens with me: Patricia and Milton Clauser of New Mexico, heirloom roses; Ann Cooper of Colorado, wildlife garden; Adele Dawson of Vermont, herb and vegetable garden; Gail, John, and Kathy Gallagher of Florida, child's garden; Carolyn Jabs of New Hampshire, bird sanctuary and woodland garden; Arvind and Bhadra Fancy of California, edible landscape and East Indian vegetable garden; Elwin Meader of New Hampshire, edible research garden; Patricia Turner of New Mexico, heirloom rose garden; and Sandra and Robert Wheeler of Oregon, meadow planting and edible garden.

The actual crafting of this book has received care and attention from a number of people. Maggie Gage, editor and garden writer, provided invaluable tutelage and groundbreaking work on my first book, much of which is reflected here. Larry Breed, proofreader and English language maven, spent hours making sure the text was correct. Ray Ten rendered the diagrams of the many gardens with a sure hand and gave them his special style. Thanks also go to Laura Creasy, Dayna Breeden, Hetty Williams, and Stephanie Disman for clerical support. Special thanks go to Diana Landau of Sierra Club Books, to Carolyn Robertson, and to Jim Robertson and the staff of The Yolla Bolly Press, Barbara Youngblood, Juliana Yoder, and Aaron Johnson, who gathered all the elements and gave the book form.

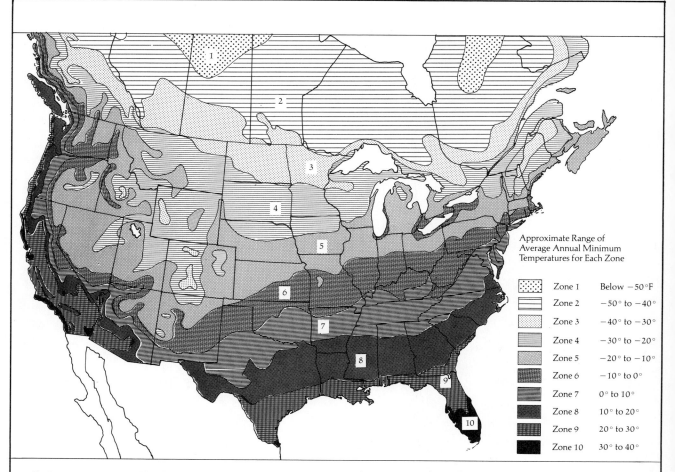

Approximate Range of
Average Annual Minimum
Temperatures for Each Zone

	Zone 1	Below −50°F
	Zone 2	−50° to −40°
	Zone 3	−40° to −30°
	Zone 4	−30° to −20°
	Zone 5	−20° to −10°
	Zone 6	−10° to 0°
	Zone 7	0° to 10°
	Zone 8	10° to 20°
	Zone 9	20° to 30°
	Zone 10	30° to 40°

It is critical to choose the right plant for the climate. This map of hardiness zones in the United States (adapted from a map prepared by the U.S. Department of Agriculture) is helpful when you start selecting your plants. Most garden texts refer to this map. To determine which plants are native to your area, however, you'll need to know more than simply how hardy a plant may be. Look at the map on page 9 for more information on which plants may be well adapted to your garden.

ZONE MAP

Bibliography

American Orchid Society. *Handbook on Orchid Culture.* Cambridge, Mass.: American Orchid Society, 1982. A booklet covering many of the basics.

Bienz, Darrel R. *The Why and How of Home Horticulture.* San Francisco: W.H. Freeman, 1980. A comprehensive collection of information on basic plant care. The book answers most of the horticultural questions that the average gardener might ask.

Brookes, John. *Room Outside: A New Approach to Garden Design.* New York: Penguin Books, 1979. This book places the garden where it belongs—as part of the family's living space. Examples of livable gardens are given.

Brooklyn Botanic Garden Handbooks. *Gardening with Wild Flowers.* No. 38. Brooklyn, N.Y.: Brooklyn Botanic Garden. How to incorporate wildflowers in your garden. This handbook is available for a small charge from Brooklyn Botanic Garden, 1000 Washington Avenue, Brooklyn, NY 11225.

_____. *Roses.* Vol. 6, no. 1. Brooklyn, N.Y.: Brooklyn Botanic Garden, 1980. A good, inexpensive basic book on rose growing.

Brown, Marc. *Your First Garden Book.* Boston: Little, Brown and Company, 1981. A book of garden projects and delights for children.

Bruce, Hal. *How to Grow Wildflowers and Wild Shrubs and Trees in Your Own Garden.* New York: Alfred A. Knopf, 1976. Valuable cultural and source information. East Coast oriented from an environmentalist's viewpoint. This text includes an encyclopedia of wildflowers and their sources.

Bryan, John E., and Castle, Coralie. *The Edible Ornamental Garden.* San Francisco: 101 Productions, 1974. The authors give numerous suggestions of plants to use and ways to enjoy your garden.

Bubel, Nancy. *The Seed Starter's Handbook.* Emmaus, Pa.: Rodale Press, 1978. Basic information on how to start most plants from seed as well as valuable botanical information on how to select and save your own seeds. A must for seed savers.

Burnett, Frances Hodgson. *The Secret Garden.* New York: Lippincott, 1938. A classic story that I must have heard or read numbers of times. A wonderful, imaginative trip set in a garden.

Carr, Anna. *Rodale's Color Handbook of Garden Insects.* Emmaus, Pa.: Rodale Press, 1979. A valuable source that will help you identify the insects in your garden—both the friends and the foes.

Cocannouer, Joseph A. *Weeds—Guardians of the Soil.* Old Greenwich, Conn.: The Devin-Adair Company, 1980. The author presents an unusual view of weeds: he praises them. He demonstrates how controlled weeds can give you insight into the composition of your soil, enrich your diet, control erosion, and improve soil fertility.

Creasy, Rosalind R. *The Complete Book of Edible Landscaping.* San Francisco: Sierra Club Books, 1982. How to use edible plants for beauty in the garden. It covers fruits and vegetables for the whole country.

Crockett, James Underwood, and Allen, Oliver E. *Wildflower Gardening*. Alexandria, Va.: Time-Life Books, 1977. A general view of the subject, with specific information on a number of wildflower species.

Damrosch, Barbara. *Theme Gardens*. New York: Workman Publishing, 1982. This book includes the plans for a marvelous old rose garden, a butterfly garden, and a hummingbird garden.

Davison, Verne E. *Attracting Birds from the Prairies to the Atlantic*. Thomas Crowell Co., 1967. This book provides good information on more than 400 species of birds.

Diamond, Denise. *Living with the Flowers*. New York: Quill, 1982. This book literally brings flowers into your life. It covers the subjects of edible flowers, how to dry flowers, gardening with flowers, even flower fairies.

Diekelmann, John, and Schuster, Robert. *Natural Landscaping, Designing with Native Plant Communities*. New York: McGraw-Hill Book Co., 1982. Basic information on landscaping with natural ecosystems, including prairies.

Dillon, Gordon W. *American Orchid Society, Beginner's Handbook*. Cambridge, Mass.: American Orchid Society, 1981. A fairly detailed book on most aspects of orchid growing.

Duncan, Wilbur H., and Foote, Leonard E. *Wildflowers of the Southeastern United States*. Athens, Ga.: University of Georgia Press, 1975. A useful guide for identifying wildflowers.

Du Pont, Elizabeth N. *Landscaping with Native Plants in the Middle-Atlantic Region*. Chadds Ford, Pa.: Brandywine Conservancy, 1978. A valuable resource for gardeners wanting a woodland garden on the Atlantic coast.

Fell, Derek. *Vegetables: How to Select, Grow, and Enjoy*. Tucson, Ariz.: H.P. Books, 1982. A marvelous compendium of basic vegetable growing.

Foster, Ruth. *Landscaping That Saves Energy Dollars*. New York: David McKay Co., 1978. A detailed text covering the many ways that landscaping can help cut energy bills.

Gessert, Kate Rogers. *The Beautiful Food Garden*. New York: Van Nostrand Reinhold Co., 1983. Gessert's book covers in great detail how to landscape with edibles and combine flowers and vegetables, as well as selections of the most beautiful vegetables and herbs.

Griffiths, Trevor. *My World of Old Roses*. London: Whitcoulls, 1983. A delightful book that covers the whole range of old roses.

Harrington, Geri. *Grow Your Own Chinese Vegetables*. New York: Collier Books, 1978. Definitely the complete word on how to grow Oriental vegetables and herbs in this country.

Hartmann, Hudson T., and Kester, Dale E. *Plant Propagation—Principles and Practices*. 3rd. ed. Englewood Cliffs, N.J.: Prentice-Hall, 1975. This book provides detailed information on the propagation of plants by seed, layering, grafting, and cutting.

Holm, LeRoy G. et al. *The World's Worst Weeds*. Honolulu: The University Press of Hawaii, 1977. A technical description of agricultural weed problems.

Jabs, Carolyn. *The Heirloom Gardener*. San Francisco: Sierra Club Books, 1984. The best and most complete book on the subject of the extinction of domestic edible plants. A must for gardeners who want to become involved with heirloom plants and seed saving.

James, Theodore, Jr. *The Gourmet Garden*. New York: E.P. Dutton, 1983. Extensive information on many superior types and varieties of vegetables and fruits.

Jeavons, John. *How to Grow More Vegetables*. Palo Alto, Calif.: Ecology Action of the Midpeninsula, 1974. A primer on French intensive gardening.

Jeavons, John, and Leler, Robin. *The Seed Finder*. Willits, Calif.: Jeavons-Leler, 1983. The key to growing superior vegetables is knowing where to get the seeds. The authors have done a service to gardeners by providing information on where to get many of the best vegetable seed varieties.

Jekyll, Gertrude. *Color Schemes for the Flower Garden*. Rev. ed. Salem, N.H.: The Ayer Co., 1983. Jekyll has profoundly influenced the modern garden. This revised classic can give you hours of pleasure, helping you to create a living painting.

Koopowitz, Harold, and Kay, Hilary. *Plant Extinction—A Global Crisis*. Washington, D.C.: Stone Wall Press, 1983. The best book for concerned homeowners. It gives extensive information about our endangered ecosystem and speaks extensively about invasive weed species.

Kruckeberg, Arthur R. *Gardening with Native Plants of the Pacific Northwest*. Seattle: University of Washington Press, 1982. A great resource for northwesterners, this book includes growing information for the Northwest as well as detailed information on species for the garden.

Larcom, Joy. *The Salad Garden*. New York: The Viking Press, 1984. A fantastic book that gives all the information you could ever want about salad vegetables. You will never again be without a salad garden of some sort.

Lenz, Lee W., and Dourley, John. *California Native Trees and Shrubs for Garden and Environmental Use in Southern California and Adjacent Areas*. Claremont, Calif.: Rancho Santa Ana Botanic Garden, 1981. This book is excellent for the gardener who is just beginning to use native plants.

Logsdon, Gene, and the editors of *Organic Gardening and Farming*. *The Gardener's Guide to Better Soil*. Emmaus, Pa.: Rodale Press, 1975. This book covers the subject in an uncomplicated and enjoyable way, emphasizing that a rewarding garden experience and healthy carefree plants begin with good garden soil.

Midda, Sara. *In and Out of the Garden*. New York: Workman Publishing, 1981. A poetic and visual delight for all people who love living things.

Miller, G. Tyler, Jr. *Living in the Environment*. Belmont, Calif.: Wadsworth Publishing, 1982. A comprehensive text on environmental theory and practice. A must for those who were educated before environmental studies were required in the school curriculum.

Mohlenbrock, Robert H. *Where Have All the Wildflowers Gone?* New York: Macmillan Co., 1983. An excellent discussion of the wildflower problem.

Mooney, Pat Roy. *Seeds of the Earth*. Ottawa, Canada: Inter Pares, 1979. A global look at the problem of the shrinking gene pool of edible plants.

Morash, Marian. *The Victory Garden Cookbook*. New York: Alfred A. Knopf, 1982. My favorite vegetable cookbook.

National Wildlife Federation. *Gardening with Wildlife*. Washington, D.C.: National Wildlife Federation, 1974. A comprehensive book on the subject of gardening with wildlife. A must!

Nichols, Stan, and Entine, Lynn. *Prairie Primer*. Madison: University of Wisconsin—Extension, 1978. A marvelous little book for beginners that has all the basics.

Niehaus, Theodore F., and Ripper, Charles L. *A Field Guide to Pacific States Wildflowers*. Boston: Houghton Mifflin, 1976. This book is helpful in identifying wildflowers

Northern, Rebecca Tyson. *Home Orchid Growing*. 3rd ed. New York: Van Nostrand

Reinhold Company, 1970. This book is a classic in its field, and if you have only one orchid-growing book, this should be it.

Organic Gardening and Farming editorial staff. *Gourmet Gardening.* Edited by Anne Moyer Halpin. Emmaus, Pa.: Rodale Press, 1978. Specific information on how to grow many unusual and superior vegetables.

Ortho Books, Chevron Chemical Company editorial staff. *All About Perennials.* San Francisco: Ortho Books, 1981. This book is primarily about water-loving nonnative plants; however, it has valuable information about how to work with perennial flower borders and flower color.

_____. *How to Attract Birds.* San Francisco: Ortho Books, 1983. Extensive information on birds and the plants they prefer for food and shelter.

_____. *The World of Cactuses and Succulents.* San Francisco: Ortho Books, 1977. How to grow, select, and maintain cactuses and succulents.

Oregon Orchid Society. *Your First Orchids and How to Grow Them.* Portland: Oregon Orchid Society, 1977. An inexpensive and pleasant way to get your feet wet.

Pavel, Margaret Brandstrom. *Gardening with Color—Ideas for Planning and Planting with Annuals, Perennials, and Bulbs.* San Francisco: Ortho Books, 1977. This book describes how to use flowering plants in the garden.

Perry, Bob. *Trees and Shrubs for Dry California Landscapes.* San Dimas, Calif.: Land Design Publishing, 1981. Valuable information about drought-tolerant plants; color prints.

Peterson, Roger Tory, and McKenny, Margaret. *A Field Guide to Wildflowers of Northeastern and North Central North America.* Boston: Houghton Mifflin, 1968. An excellent field guide.

Rickett, Harold William. *Wild Flowers of the United States.* 6 vols. New York: McGraw-Hill Book Co., 1966-70. This is the perfect book for wildflower mavens.

Robinson, William. *The Wild Garden.* Rev. ed. London: Century Publishing, 1983. A revised classic that is particularly appropriate today. Robinson's outrage at the traditional formal borders and controlled gardens of his day inspired him to expound his theory of gardening, one that respects and uses native and wild plants. While most of the plants discussed in this book are for English gardens, the ideas and designs are appropriate everywhere.

Rock, Harold W. *Prairie Propagation Handbook.* Hales Corners, Wis.: Milwaukee County Department of Parks, 1981. This basic text is necessary for those who are interested in maintaining a prairie garden.

Rothschild, Miriam, and Farrell, Clive. *The Butterfly Gardener.* London: Michael Joseph, 1983. A must for butterfly lovers. It even covers raising butterflies in captivity.

Santa Barbara Botanic Garden. *Native Plants for Southern California Gardens.* No. 12. Santa Barbara: Santa Barbara Botanic Garden, 1969. Detailed information on California native plants and the growing conditions they prefer.

Saratoga Horticultural Foundation. *Selected California Native Plants with Commercial Sources.* 3rd ed. Saratoga, Calif.: Saratoga Horticultural Foundation, 1983. This book is particularly helpful in finding sources for the native plants you want.

Schuler, Stanley, and Schuler, Elizabeth Meriwether. *Preserving the Fruits of the Earth.* New York: Dial Press, 1973. A book that is hard to find but worth looking for. It covers in detail how to preserve nearly everything.

Skelsey, Alice, and Huckaby, Gloria. *Growing Up Green.* New York: Workman Publishing, 1973. A guide for parents and children and how they can share the wonder of living things. A gem!

Smith, J. Robert, and Smith, Beatrice S. *The Prairie Garden*. Madison: University of Wisconsin Press, 1980. A useful book that describes in detail seventy native prairie plants and how to use them in your yard. In addition, it details how to collect seeds, raise your own plants, and maintain a prairie.

Smith, Ken. *Western Home Landscaping*. Tucson, Ariz.: H.P. Books, 1978. A helpful book for home landscapers. It has quite a bit of information on drought-tolerant plants and how to put in a drip irrigation system.

Southern Living editorial Staff. *Southern Living—Growing Vegetables and Herbs*. Birmingham, Ala.: Oxmoor House, 1984. This marvelous book discusses vegetable culture and cooking techniques for southern gardeners.

Sunset Books editorial staff. *New Western Garden Book*. Menlo Park, Calif.: Lane Publishing Co., 1979. This book is a must for all western gardeners; it's considered the bible of West Coast gardening.

———. *Sunset Italian Cookbook*. Menlo Park, Calif.: Lane Publishing Co., 1974. A good basic Italian cookbook.

Vilmorin-Andrieux, MM. *The Vegetable Garden*. Palo Alto, Calif.: Jeavons-Leler Press.

Reprint 1976. A marvelous reprint of a classic that was first printed in 1885. It is a description of the old varieties, with information on how to grow hundreds of them. I counted fifty-five pages on peas alone.

Waters, Alive. *Chez Panisse Menu Cookbook*. New York: Random House, 1982. An inspiring cookbook by an author who feels that fresh, superior, home-grown produce is the starting point for outstanding cuisine.

White, Katherine S. *Onward and Upward in the Garden*. New York: Farrar, Straus & Giroux, 1979. One woman's delightful view of gardening.

Williams, Brian. *Orchids for Everyone*. New York: Crown Publishers, 1980. A beautiful book showing 200 orchids in color with extensive practical advice.

Williams, John G., and Williams, Andrew E. *Field Guide to Orchids of North America*. New York: Universe Books, 1983. A useful guide for looking at or photographing orchids in the wild.

Wilson, William H. W. *Landscaping with Wildflowers and Native Plants*. San Francisco: Ortho Books, Chevron Chemical Company, 1984. A most valuable and up-to-date book covering in detail most of the many ecosystems in this country. The book contains numerous lists of native plants to choose for your landscape as well as information on how to plant and maintain them.

Index

Italicized page references indicate illustrations.

A

Acacia melanoxylon, 18
Acer species, 38, 101
Acres of Orchids, 119, 124
Actinindia arguta, 143
African daisy, *31*
Agave deserti, 102
Ailanthus altissima, 18
Akebia quinata, 101
Albizia Fulibrissin, 101
Alcea rosea, 102, 180
Allium schoenoprasum, 102
Allium tuberosum, 180
Aloe polyphylla, 74
Aloe species, 62
Alpine strawberry, 136, 137
Amalia orchid, 74
Amaranth, 136
Amaranthus species, 101
Amelanchier species, 38, 101
American cranberry bush, 101
Amorpha canescens, 49
Andropogon Gerardii, 48
Andropogon scoparius, 49
Anemone lancifolia, 32
Anemone patens, var. *Wolfgangiana,* 49
Anemone: tree, 61; woodland, *32*
Anethum graveolens, 102, 180
Annuals: for birds, 101; for butterflies, 102; for cutting, 162; in meadow garden, 28
Aquilegia canadensis, 22
Aquilegia species, 101
Arctostaphylos, 61
Artotheca calendula, 62
Arctotis species, 62
Ariocarpus agavoides, 74
Asclepias tuberosa, 30, 49
Aster novae-angliae, 49
Aster species, 49, 101, 102
'Austin' orchid, 102
Avocado, 134
Aztekium Ritteri, 74

B

Bachelor's button, 101
Backyard Wildlifer, The, 93
Bacterial blight, 84
Bamboo, 18, 134-135
Banana, 136
Baptisia leucantha, 50
Baptisia leucophaea, 49
Barnes, Carl, 79
Bean: 'Dutch White' runner, 151; haricots verts, 137; 'Royal Burgundy', 151; 'Royalty', 151; yard-long, 136
Beans: diseases of, 84; freezing seeds of, 84; saving, 84
Bean tepee, *152*
Beet, 135
Bellis perennis, 18
Berberis Thunbergii, 18
Bermuda grass, 18
Betula species, 38, 101
Biennial vegetables, 83
Big bluestem, 48
Bird-food violet, 50
Bird houses, *91, 94*
Bitter melon, 136, 138
Bittersweet, 101; Oriental, 15, 17, 18
Blackberry, 17; Himalayan, 18
Black-eyed susan, *29, 101*
Blazing-star, 49
Blueberry, 102
Blue-eyed grass, 50
Blue vanda orchid, 74
Borago officinalis, 180
Border: chaparral flower, *57-58*; mixed, *175*; perennial, *175*; prairie, 47
Bottle gentian, *71*
Bougainvillea species, 62
Bracken fern, 18
Brassia Edvah Loo, *99*
Brazilian pepper, 15, 17, 18
Broadleaf cycad, 74
Broccoli, 'Romanesco', *139*

Viola tricolor, 180
Virginia creeper, 101

W

Watercress, 18
Watering of chaparral garden, *59*
Water for wildlife, 94-96
Weeds, 13, 14-18; controlling, 17; definition of, 14; as foes in natural areas, 14; guidelines for identifying, 17; in a meadow garden, 28
White Rugosa rose, *100*
White wild indigo, *50*
Wildflower seed mixes, 15, 17; sources of, 33, *53*
Wildflowers: for cutting, 161, 162; in a woodland garden, 40
Wildlife: needs of, 91, 94-96; protection from, 103
Wildlife garden, 89-105; diagram of, *95;* planning of, 94-96; plants for, 96, 101-102
Willow, 102
Winterberry, 101
Winter creeper, 101

Wisteria species, 102
Witch hazel, 101
Woodland anemone, *32*
Woodland garden, 35-43; diagram of, *41;* guidelines for converting existing garden to, 37; guidelines for starting new, 37; planning of, 36-37; size of, 35; soil for, 37
Woodthrush, *97*
Wreaths, 163

Y

Yard-long bean, 136
Yards, 159
Yellow bedstraw, 18
Yucca species, *65*

Z

Zauschneria californica, 61
Zinnia linearis, 178
Zinnia species, 102
Zone map, 186
Zucchini, 136; 'Gold Rush', *161, 165*